WHAT YOU DON'T KNOW ABOUT **RETIREMENT PLANNING** CAN HURT YOU

Financial strategies to guide you
down the mountain in retirement
from an expert Financial Professional

DAN WHITE

SECOND EDITION

FOREWORDS BY ED SLOTT, CPA AND RETIREMENT EXPERT AND DR. JACK MARRION, D.M.

FUTURE
PUBLISHING

SOUTHFIELD, MI

Published by Future Publishing, Inc.
Southfield, MI

Project coordination by Jenkins Group, Inc. • www.BookPublishing.com

Interior layout by Andrea Reider

Printed in the United States of America
26 25 24 23 22 • 5 4 3 2 1

To my wife, Cindy, for her love and support throughout my career, along with her understanding of the hours that I have kept.

To my four children, Jessica, Justin, Dylan, and Zachary who in their unique way have kept me grounded, never getting too high or too low with the cyclical swings of our business.

Contents

Contents

Foreword to the Second Edition

By Ed Slott, CPA and retirement expert

You save your whole life, but then when it comes to retirement, you realize something is missing – a plan for what comes next. You now have one in your hands.

What's nice about this book is its easiness. It really flows well and by the end, you realize everything you were wondering or worrying about is covered. You'll learn practical planning tips and be alerted to traps and mistakes to watch out for.

Financial advisor and author Dan White has been studying these critical planning issues for several years with our advanced retirement tax planning education group *"Ed Slott's Elite IRA Advisor Group*^{SM}*."* This team receives the nation's highest level of continuous individual retirement account (IRA) distribution training for financial advisors. And this is *in addition to* Dan's many years serving clients with the same concerns you have.

Dan covers everything you need to plan for in retirement and beyond, but without all the overly complicated technical aspects that most books on this subject are filled with. That doesn't mean that anything is left out. In fact, it's just the opposite. What you need to know is in here, with simple explanations that empower you to finally understand concepts that you were probably afraid to address because they seemed too complicated, which resulted in inaction and even more worry about the future.

Once you find yourself grasping the issues better, you're more likely to successfully address your planning needs. That is the biggest benefit you'll find when you go through this gem of a book. After Dan's masterful explanations, he often follows them up with real-life examples from his years of helping clients just like you, and even examples from his own family. I find his stories engaging and relatable. I think you will too.

You'll be surprised at how much you learn, especially when Dan wraps it up to help you understand the most essential points. For example, early in the book when explaining how important income in retirement is, you'll find this line: "In the end, you have to understand that all your assets essentially are there to provide income at some point." That really drives the point home and gives you a better idea of how to create an income plan as you go through the rest of the book.

Dan addresses thorny issues like what to do when you have competing objectives. For example, you want your retirement money to grow, but you also want safety. You want guaranteed income, but don't want your money tied up. What to do? This is a fine balancing act, but Dan shows you how to prioritize your planning goals to reflect on what matters most.

This book is a guide to planning principles, an educational resource to revisit as your life changes, and a gift to share with family and friends. The reason is Dan. He calls himself a "financial educator," which is why the book is so easy to learn from.

This book also stresses the value of working with a retirement specialist. In my opinion, it's an absolute need. The tax rules involved are complex, often rigid, and unforgiving. You may not get many second chances if costly mistakes are made.

In this book you'll learn how to avoid the worst retirement miscues by reading some of the financial horror stories included. One stark example is the story of Bruce Friedman, whose wife suddenly died. He then found out he was not her beneficiary because the beneficiary form was not updated from years ago before they were married. This resulted in a $1 million loss. After reading this, I think anyone would be highly motivated to run and check their IRA and other retirement plan beneficiary forms!

The book covers a wide array of retirement concerns from Social Security claiming options (Dan says that there are 567 ways for a couple to claim social security retirement benefits – yikes!), to long-term care and estate planning (including a very well-done explanation of all the essential estate planning documents you should have). He covers all the tax traps with those pesky RMDs (required minimum distributions) which can cost you plenty if you run afoul of these archaic tax rules.

Dan covers the benefits of tax-free retirement savings through either Roth IRAs or life insurance as a key planning item that can benefit everyone, especially if you see the writing on the wall for Congress raising tax rates in the very near future.

Dan also points out the risks of longevity and stock market exposure. His advice on the importance of guaranteed income and the use of annuities removes all the doubt, suspicion, and fear that sometimes surrounds these products by highlighting the ultimate goal, which is to provide peace of mind.

But to balance that advice, he also warns that you don't want to rely solely on guaranteed income, because you may need quick access to funds for financial emergencies. This all makes a lot of sense, and after reading this book, you'll probably see how this type of planning can fit your personal needs and the needs of your loved ones.

Even if you think you have most of this covered, read the book anyway. You might be surprised at what you'll learn. There may be unaddressed areas in your plan. Reading this book will better prepare you to deal with that now, especially in light of recent tax law changes, like the SECURE Act, which is covered at the end of the book.

Dan asks, "When did you last take your retirement plan to a specialist?" The answer will be a big factor in your retirement success. Since you have this book, you've already taken the first step. Now it's time to complete your plan. The book has you covered there too by providing some incredibly powerful advice (see the end of the chapter on procrastination).

It's time to get started. You have a great guide in Dan White (or a "Sherpa" as he calls it). He's right — what you don't know about retirement planning really *can* hurt you. Read this book, prepare well, then look forward to less worry and more fun for your retirement years. Good luck!

Ed Slott, CPA, and retirement expert
Author and founder of www.irahelp.com
Founder of *Ed Slott's Elite IRA Advisor Group*[SM]
October 28, 2021

Foreword

By Dr. Jack Marrion, D.M.

Dan's excellent book hits on several financial themes that simply don't get enough attention. One is that retirement planning is an active process, because often real life doesn't follow the plan. Dan reminds us that a 50% loss in the value of our assets means a 100% return is needed to simply get us back to even. Also, a person should never forget inflation is lurking and unless steps are taken, it can cut into quality of life down the road. Another theme is his focus on diversity. I've read far too many books where the writer talks as if there is only one solution and ignores everything else. Dan takes a holistic approach and mentions equities, bonds, annuities, insurance solutions, and using the bank. His chapter on Social Security doesn't bash it (as some do), but talks about maximizing Social Security benefits and minimizing taxes on those benefits. Speaking of taxes, this book talks about realistic ways to minimize and possibly avoid not only income taxes during retirement, but estate taxes as well.

A point that hit home with me was Dan's guidance on ensuring our plans for life and retirement happen. He's experienced how an early death can disrupt life's plans and what should have been done. He talks about the real-world possibility that long-term nursing care will be needed at some point. And he outlines why the security of a guaranteed income often makes sense.

Finally, what I really like are the stories. This book wasn't written from some ivory tower, but from Dan's personal relationship with the couple where the husband had Crohn's disease, talking about his grandfather's retirement, the nurse he helped get a bigger Social Security check, and the couple with the unexpected job loss. I won't give away what Dan told the Fox Business News reporter when asked, "What is the single biggest mistake retirement savers make?" Instead, I'll end by quoting from Dan's approach to planning – hope is not a strategy.

Dr. Jack Marrion, D.M.
Jack Marrion is president of Advantage Compendium providing research and consulting services to financial firms and has thrice been asked to address the National Association of Insurance Commissioners. He has authored six books on topics that include understanding fixed annuities, retirement income planning, and behavioral finance. Prior to forming

Advantage Compendium, Dr. Marrion was formerly vice president of a life insurance company and vice president of an investment banking firm. He received an MBA from the University of Missouri and his doctorate focusing on cognitive bias in decision-making formed a new paradigm in effectively working with consumers. Neither Dr. Marrion nor Advantage Compendium sell or endorse any financial product.

Chapter One

How a Small Amount of Time Can Derail Your Retirement

I'm not your average retirement planning expert. A prime example of that is my response when people ask to see my portfolio. The first thing I do is show them a photo of my family, because they're my real investment. Everything is done with them as my primary focus.

Sure, I have money invested in various places, but it's all done with my family in mind. After all, isn't that why you wake up every day and work hard? For me, and many others, it's all to make a better life for our families.

That's been my philosophy since my wife Cindy and I first married more than 37 years ago. It's a long-term outlook that centers on vision and values, and my clients tend to agree with it. With family at the center of everything, the stakes are high, so it's important to get it right. That's why people come to see me. They realize we have one chance at retirement success, so it's worth consulting an expert.

At the core of retirement planning is time, and the understanding that time is our most important commodity. Money comes and goes. People have become rich, lost it all, then became rich again. But time is different. Unlike money, you can't get time back once it's spent.

In a retirement sense, that means we must realize the importance of creating a plan and sticking with it. Save *over time*. Pay ourselves first *over time*. Be smart with expenses *over time*. If you're diligent and consistent in executing your plan, you'll realize your dream retirement – or something very close.

Timing is just as important. For example, *when* we started saving, *when* we started working, *when* we retire – all of these can have a big effect on retirement. Getting to your ideal retirement is done over the course of an entire career. But, events that unfold in a relatively short time can spoil a retirement if you're unprepared. Knowing all that, it justifiably causes concern among retirement savers. And let's face it, there's a lot that can keep you up at night when it comes to retirement.

If you're anything like me, the reason you're concerned about your retirement is your family and its wellbeing. For me, it's these people right here. (See family photo on next page.)

We love our families through and through. That said, in my opinion, the most popular bank in the U.S. today is The Bank of Mom & Dad. A lot of retirees will

Dan White (center) and his family

come in to my office and say, "we're empty nesters." But then they get the phone call – "Hey mom, my marriage isn't going too well." Or, "Hey dad, my business isn't doing well, and I need to move back home. By the way, I'm bringing the three grandkids with me."

Those retirees thought their nest was empty and now they're playing with a full house again. So, that makes mom and dad's assets, like individual retirement accounts (IRAs) and other such accounts, very important to the family overall. Because in today's economic environment, you never know how long you'll have to take care of your family.

But hey, the stock market has been going well for a while, so it doesn't matter, right? Everyone is feeling good about the market. We're experiencing all-time highs regularly. Well, the market can't stay hot forever.

Given the context of family we just discussed, what I'm trying to illustrate is the potential cost of a minor downturn.

The fact is, if you're in the stock market, you're taking risks. You're doing that to get a higher rate of return, primarily because we can't earn much at banks anymore. So if you're trying to hit a higher rate of return, what's the goal on an annual basis? Is it 6%, 8%, 10% or more? Before 2000, everyone would've said 10%, and today I think most would gladly take a 10% return. But is chasing 10% per year worth it?

In the chart below, we see an investment in the market over the course of a few years. Let's say it's part of Janice's retirement portfolio. Janice is nearing retirement, but is still about five years away.

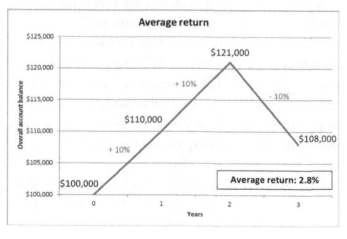

Source: Dan White and Associates

In year one, she earned 10% on her investment and life was good. Why would she get out now? Her investment just went up in value. Why not ride it out?

We all hear to buy low and sell high. But how many people do that? Hardly any. Why don't people do that? When you think about it, it goes against human nature. Does anybody wake up on a Monday morning and say, "Hey honey, I'm feeling like a million bucks, call the doctor!" Consequently, we never think about exiting the market when we're making money.

So the second year arrives, and Janice is rewarded with another 10% return. Now she's up to $121,000 and life continues to be grand. There's no way she's exiting the market now.

But then Janice hits a little bump in year three. Maybe it's a tsunami in the Far East, an oil spill in the Gulf of Mexico, maybe a pandemic, or something else she has no control over. As a result, the market falls 10%.

My question is, what was her average return over those three years? It was 2.8%. The point is, if you're in the market, you're taking risks to get that higher rate of return. But when you hit that little bump and it knocks your average return down to what used to be a good savings account rate, it makes you wonder if it's worth it.

Janice's case is just one example, and it's not like she lost a ton of money during that time. But it shows how a bit of time can hinder a retirement savings effort. Now, other folks have had much worse luck.

Date	S&P 500 Value
Jan. 1, 2000 *(dotcom bubble)*	1,429
Sept. 9, 2002	815
Oct. 9, 2007 *(height before credit crisis)*	1,565
Mar. 9, 2009	676
Jan. 2, 2013	1,426
Jan. 12, 2017	2,270

For instance, some retirees sustained negative, or in the best case, stagnant returns for a decade. It happened recently, from 2000-2010, or what I like to call "the lost decade."

In 2000, the S&P 500 opened at 1,429. But, soon we hit the "dotcom bubble." If you rode that out to its low point in 2002 when the S&P 500 hit 815, you would've lost 45% of your investment in less than three years. If you had a broker then, he or she likely said, "hang in there, it'll come back in time!"

And, the S&P 500 did come back five years later in 2007, when it closed at 1,565. Up until about 2013, that was the all-time high. But in October 2007, we suffered from the credit crisis/subprime mortgage bubble, and the market tanked. The S&P 500 dropped to a paltry 676 in less than two years. This time, it meant a 57% loss in just 17 months, and the end of Bear Sterns, Lehman Brothers and Merrill Lynch.

What does your broker say this time? "Ride it out. You don't want to sell at the bottom.

You hung in there, and all was well, because in January 2013, we made it back to the same levels as 2000. We finally broke even. And now, we're hitting all-time highs with some regularity.

So all is good, right? Well, it's a good news/bad news story.

The good news is you're up 55% in the stock market from 2013-2017. A 55% return in four years (about 14% per year) isn't so bad, is it? I think not.

The bad news is you're up 55% in the stock market from 2000-2017. Clearly, that run from 2000-2010 did nobody any favors, and a 55% return in 17 years isn't that great.

It begs the question – where do you think we're going next in the market?

The problem is it's quite difficult to recover from big market drops. The chart below paints a grim picture. If your portfolio suffers a big hit from a down market, it can be catastrophic, if not fatal.

Probability of Recovery							
Portfolio Loss	Needed Cumulative Gain to Restore Loss	Percentage Chance of Recovery From Loss Within...					
		1 year	2 years	3 years	4 years	5 years	10 years
-10%	11.1%	52.5%	74.4%	81.6%	78.4%	77.8%	93.5%
-20%	25%	25.0%	48.7%	68.4%	67.6%	72.2%	93.5%
-50%	100%	0.0%	0.0%	7.9%	13.5%	36.1%	80.6%

Probabilities calculated from historical returns of S&P 500 Index over past 40 years.
Source: *The Math of Gains and Losses, Craig Israelson, Ph.D.*

If you suffer a 10% hit one year, you have to gain 11% to recover. If it's a 20% hit, you must come up

25% the next year. And if it's half of your portfolio, it will have to double in value to restore the loss.

Let's think about it another way. If you made 10%, how would your life change?

Not much. You'd feel good, sure. But you probably wouldn't buy the new Maserati with cash or go on a cruise.

Now, what if you lost 50%? How would your life change? It would change a lot. You'd be devastated.

If it happened early in life, time could help you recover. If it happened late in the game, it might mean you never retire.

The main point is it will take time to recover from big downturns, if recovery happens at all. We're not factoring inflation into the mix in this example, which would add difficulty to the situation. If your portfolio recovered, a decade on, things will cost more. So, are you really breaking even?

Given how important retirement is, planning for it should be a priority for everyone. Sadly, it is not. As we saw in this chapter, exposure to market risk, poor timing and difficult recoveries can crush a retirement portfolio. Despite decades of saving, just a few bad years can be detrimental to a retirement.

But it doesn't have to be that way. It's possible to live your dream retirement, even if the market is going crazy. You can avoid losing both time and money by properly planning for retirement. But almost like they say on those detective shows – what you don't know can, and will, hurt you.

When my staff and I see when people retire happy, it's the best. When they have income, they have peace of mind.

One of my favorite stories is from nearly a decade ago. A husband and wife came to visit me, and the husband had Crohn's disease for about 50 years. We set up a retirement plan with guaranteed income that would set them up for life. But, those income sources were meant to be used a little later in life. So, they'd defer that income for about a decade and rely on other assets in the meantime.

Well, the husband was still working, and they were doing all the right things with Social Security. Being the same age, the plan was to activate the guaranteed income when they both hit age 70. Unfortunately, he passed away when he was 68.

That wasn't in the plan, obviously. As a result, the wife lost a Social Security benefit. And that left her with a 50% monthly income gap to cover. If she could make it to age 70, she'd have guaranteed income for life and be fine. But she was 68 at the time.

So, we pivoted slightly and took advantage of some of her other assets for a couple years. She had other accounts, though they did not have big balances. Still, she drew those down over the next couple years.

When she turned 70, she came to see me. She looked nervous and I asked her if everything was all right. She said she was just about out of money and struggling. I wished her a happy birthday and smiled. Then I said we were activating her guaranteed income.

When I mentioned how it would more than cover all her expenses, she cried. She then said the best thing she and her husband ever did was attend one of my dinner seminars!

That couple benefited from planning ahead. What does that mean, exactly? It means accounting for income, insurance, asset protection, debt management, mortgage planning and more. That sounds like a lot, and it is. Our lives are a journey, and sometimes they get complicated. But our financial lives and retirement journeys are no different.

When we hit rough patches, we get help from others. That's especially true for experts in subjects we have little or no knowledge. For instance, cardiologists, mechanics, internet repair people and the like – they use deep knowledge to guide us and provide solutions.

Think of a retirement planner like a guide as well – someone who can provide ongoing valuable expertise. Since retirement is such an important journey, isn't it worth working with an expert? I mean, if you were going to climb a huge mountain, would you go solo? You'd be foolish to do that. If you did, a cold final ending is almost a certainty.

No, if you were headed on such an adventure, you'd want the best tools, information and support. If you look at the best adventurers and explorers throughout history, they usually have superb help. Follow their lead and consider enlisting expert assistance. It could make a significant difference on your retirement journey.

Chapter Two

Our Financial Lives As Mount Everest

As I said in the last chapter, I look at our financial lives as a long journey that has peaks and valleys throughout. One of the main metaphors I use to illustrate that point is Mount Everest. It's the world's tallest mountain and it's a fitting structure for our example. That's because for each of us, our finances mean the world and success is equivalent to scaling Mount Everest.

I prefer a lot of audience participation during my seminars, so sometimes I'll quiz people randomly. For instance, two people are widely credited with reaching the top of Mount Everest before anyone else. Can you name them? Here's a photo hint (see photo on the next page):

Most people get one of them right, naming Sir Edmund Hillary, the gentleman on the left in the above photo. But hardly anyone knows the other person.

It is his Sherpa guide for the excursion, Tenzing Norgay. Without him, Hillary would not have made it to the top. That's because besides providing expert guidance, Norgay also saved Hillary's life. From Hillary's obituary in the Telegraph:

But (Hillary) had a narrow escape when the ice gave way as he was moving loads up to this camp, plunging him into a crevasse. Fortunately Tenzing, who was following, thrust his ice-axe in the snow, and whipped the rope round it in good belay. It tightened just in time to prevent Hillary from being smashed to pieces at the bottom of the crevasse. Thereafter Hillary began to think of Tenzing as the ideal partner in a bid for the summit.

Every successful summit of Mount Everest uses a Sherpa guide because they're the world's best mountaineers. The Sherpa people are natives of Nepal – you could say they're literally made from mountains. Norgay and others like him were a big reason Hillary and team reached the summit in 1953.

That year is important, because a pair of climbers are suspected to have reached the top in 1921, well before Hillary and Norgay. Can you name them? Not many people get them both.

The climbers were George Mallory and Andrew Irvine. They are suspected to have reached the top in 1921. Why only "suspected"? Because they never made it down. We don't know if they made it to the top because they died on the way down. They also didn't have a Sherpa guide.

If you think of retirement day as reaching the top of your personal Mount Everest, the rest of your life is the descent. Unfortunately, much like Mallory and Irvine, most people's retirement plans fail after they retire, or on the way down the mountain.

In some ways, it's easier to get to retirement, or go up the mountain, than to stay retired. That's because if you make a mistake getting to retirement, you can keep working (if you still have a job).

But what if you make a mistake after you retire? You run out of money. When you retire, what you have is what you have. You don't get any more money going in. The faucet is turned off. That's why mistakes can be fatal to your retirement.

Knowing this, it's important to understand the differences between going up the mountain and coming down. In retirement, ascending is called accumulation, while descending is called preservation. As their names indicate, accumulation is about increasing wealth, while preservation is about protecting and harvesting it over time. The behaviors and priorities are different in each phase. What's important in accumulation becomes less so in preservation and vice versa. We'll go over these concepts more later in the book, but know there are distinct phases of retirement.

Now, just as in life, climbing a mountain contains unknown perils, surprises and moments of uncertainty. Obviously, it's easier to handle them if you're prepared. The same rings true with retirement planning. But how do you prepare for that? A big part is identifying what you know, what you don't, and then filling the gaps accordingly. Simply put, knowing our limitations helps us work towards overcoming them.

Here's a nice visual representation of the concept:

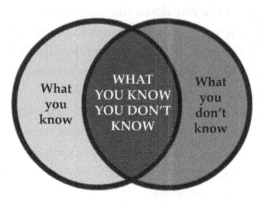

Clearly, this is also a visual way to represent the fact that nobody knows everything! Applying this solely to retirement planning, the circle sizes and overlap may vary, but the point remains that there are many unknowns.

That diagram is why so many people need help – there's so much to know and address. Still, many go the solo route when it comes to retirement planning, thinking they don't need assistance. People do the same with mountain climbing, too. But just because people do it doesn't mean it's the best choice for everyone.

For instance, even after taking inventory of your retirement planning knowledge, there's still more to the story. For instance, financial and insurance industry offerings change regularly. So do tax laws and financial regulations. Are those things on your radar?

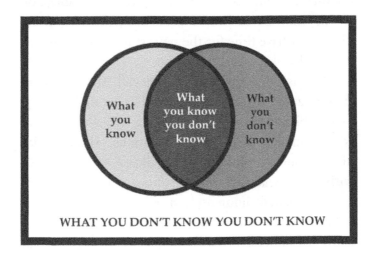

WHAT YOU DON'T KNOW YOU DON'T KNOW

Without expert help, you can't address what you *don't know* you don't know – which can be a lot! Believe me, what you don't know about retirement planning can hurt you.

This is why Sir Edmund Hillary had Tenzing Norgay with him. Norgay helped Hillary successfully navigate treacherous terrain to reach the ultimate goal. The Sherpa guide's expertise likely made the difference, because climbers who go without them tend to end in peril.

In retirement, it's very much the same. I won't say it's life or death, but what you don't know you don't know can make a big difference. There may be insurance policies, annuities, or investments that could be perfect for you. But if you don't know about them, you'll never benefit. And let's be honest, most outside the financial industry don't know what's available, nor should they. Most people are busy with their lives. They don't have time for the newest fixed index annuities or the like!

This is why you need a financial Sherpa guide. A full career in retirement is as big an undertaking as climbing Mount Everest, complete with all the accompanying trials and tribulations. If you take nothing more from this book, please at least speak with a financial professional about your retirement. You will benefit immensely from a professional who is knowledgeable and, like a Sherpa guide, can steer you away from danger and towards your ultimate goal.

Chapter Three

Common Retirement Mistakes – Are You Making Them?

One person pretends to be rich, although he has nothing; another has great wealth but goes in rags.

Proverbs 13:7

I've been in this business for more than 35 years, and I'm still motivated every day by the same thing – helping people. They don't teach financial literacy in school – they don't even teach you how to balance a checkbook. Naturally, we think people with lots of things have lots of money. But, as the Proverbs quote attests, that's not always the case. Living within your means helps create wealth. And we'd know that if we were better educated about money.

When people are done with school and start working, learning personal finance isn't high on the to-do list. The result is that almost all the mistakes in retirement stem from a lack of education. And that's how people get to their 50s and 60s but aren't ready to retire.

First and foremost, I consider myself a financial educator because it's how I can help people the most. During meetings, I like to hear about how people first learned about money. For me, that was at 11-years-old, running a newspaper delivery route. When I went to college, I managed the finances for houses I lived in. It's built from there ever since.

Many people say they learned about it after getting their first "real" job out of school. And some of the late bloomers didn't start paying bills or managing their finances until their mid-twenties! The fact is, for whatever reason, many people aren't educated on finances. Consequently, they fail at retirement. I don't mean that to be disparaging. Based on my experience, it's reality. People need help, and there are experts out there to help because people don't know what they don't know.

To be sure, even those who are financially literate and savvy can benefit from expert help. Because even when they have a good plan in place, there could be strategic blind spots.

For instance, I have a client who has done well and accumulated wealth over his lifetime. We started talking about his investments one day, and he said, "I fill the bucket." I asked what he meant. He said he socks money away – whatever the maximum allowed is, he will save that much. And then he said, "Honestly, I don't know what I'm doing, but I keep on filling that bucket."

I told him it was good he was filling the bucket – some people don't even do that. But it was my job to stop the leaks in the bucket. What are the leaks? Some include market risk, inflation, and misaligned assets. Each of these can drain a portfolio.

My client didn't think of himself as an investor, but as a saver. What was his plan? Fill the bucket. And that's fine, except he had buckets all over the place. There's no doubt he was filling the buckets, but they had several leaks until we corrected things.

Let's talk about **misaligned assets, or what I call the "dartboard approach."** This is pretty common today. I think it's because the retirement income paradigm of pensions, Social Security and personal savings doesn't exist anymore. Pensions are all but gone from the modern workforce. Social Security is there, but its longevity is anybody's guess. So, that puts the onus (and risk) on your personal savings.

As a result, people save money here, there, and everywhere. A 401(k) with one investment firm, a brokerage account someplace else, an IRA, two certificates of deposit (CDs) at two different banks – before you know it, it's hard to even keep track of them all! That means your assets aren't working to your greatest advantage.

If you can envision yourself in retirement and know what it feels like, you're more likely to make it come to fruition. I doubt that includes paying a mortgage or worrying about having enough money. But it amazes me how often I see that with people. And unfortunately, few advisors will run a report telling you these things.

In the end, you have to understand that all your assets essentially are there to provide income at some point. When I ask people where they'll draw money from in retirement and they aren't sure, I know they need help. They have no idea of their income needs in retirement or where that money will come from. That's having no plan, like tossing darts aimlessly and hoping for a bullseye.

Put another way, there's **no personal mix of growth, income, protection and liquidity**. These objectives are the pillars of personal financial planning, and if managed well, will provide for a successful retirement. However, they are at odds with each other. For instance, you can't focus on both growth (buying stocks) and protection (not buying stocks). Managing these objectives is an important part of planning, and I like to start with asking people about their priorities.

When I ask people what's most important, deep down, almost everyone wants their money to be protected. We don't want to lose our money. We worked hard for it and want it to remain ours. I get that.

What else matters? We want growth. Nobody wants to sit on the sidelines while the market is cruising. Plus, many folks aren't even sure they have enough to retire, so they *need* growth. And parking it at a bank for 0.1% or less won't work. OK, but that usually means absorbing risk for greater return, which doesn't jibe with protection.

In addition to growth and protection, we need income too. Pensions are either discounted or gone, and maybe you're not old enough for Social Security yet. Regardless, there's no denying we need income in retirement from somewhere. Thankfully, even without a pension, guaranteed income is possible.

So is there anything else we want in retirement? Yes. We want access to our assets – otherwise known as liquidity. We don't want our money tied up. We want to travel and drive recent model cars, both of which require money. Fine, but that doesn't work with a guaranteed income stream, which takes assets to fund.

So, most people want their money protected, need it to grow, want income and don't want to tie any of it up. It's very difficult for someone to set up a portfolio to satisfy four competing objectives like that. Now, I can help with all of these things. But, it's important to identify the inherent conflicts and adjust accordingly. This is why prioritizing is so important. We can find out what matters for you, and work around those wishes.

Now, something we don't wish for is the loss of a spouse. But unfortunately, **not planning for income loss due to a spouse passing away** is a huge mistake. Not only can it be personally devastating, but financially devastating to boot.

I speak from somewhat personal experience on this, as my father passed away when he was 46 years old. I was 21 at the time. My mother was 45, so I'm very cognizant of what happens when a spousal loss occurs. It's not easy on anyone in the family, and frankly, finances aren't exactly top-of-mind. This is exactly when an outside expert can provide huge value. They can handle the details and let the family deal with other things. I wish we had someone to help when my dad passed. We made it work, but it was tough. Helping people avoid that situation is one of the things I really love about my work.

When I sit down with married couples, I want to know exactly what will happen with income if either spouse passes. In other words, I want to know how much income the wife will have if the husband doesn't wake up tomorrow, and vice versa.

"But that won't happen," some people say, and use that as a crutch for not planning. But we all know funerals occur every day. Unfortunately, it's not unusual for me to sit with people and discover that when one spouse dies, the surviving spouse could stand to lose a lot of income. Sometimes it's up to $40,000 per year or more, which can be a fatal financial blow. But it doesn't have to unfold that way. There are ways to position assets so they make up for some or all of the lost income when the first spouse dies.

Some other strategies to mitigate income drops due to spousal loss include life insurance and deferred annuities. With these in place, income is triggered upon the spouse's passing. Sometimes it can even grow in value until needed. To be sure, these solutions don't ease the pain of losing a loved one. That said, they do provide some peace of mind that the financial situation is fine – and that's one less thing to worry about during a tough time.

Additionally, your beneficiary setup can make a huge difference with income after a spouse passes away. If properly configured, tax benefits can continue, and distribution requirements can be adjusted to the surviving spouse. But if you don't know that, you likely won't be prepared to take advantage. We'll talk more in more detail about beneficiaries and how to ensure your assets follow your wishes in Chapter Eight. The important thing to understand here is to plan so that if one spouse passes away, the other won't be without income.

Many of the retirement mistakes I see people make occur because of **failing to plan for inflation and living longer.** Longevity, or living so long you run out of money, is the biggest risk retirees face today.

When you think about it, longevity makes every other risk in retirement worse. The longer you live, the more likely…

…the market will crash.

…inflation will eat into the purchasing power of your fixed income.

…you will need care from somebody, in some circumstance.

Longevity is the big risk here folks.

I was at a seminar in Scottsdale, Ariz., a while back and the featured speaker discussed longevity in detail.

He said there are more than 93,000 Americans over the age of 100, and more than 6 million aged 85 or above. Clearly, we're able to live a lot longer than previous generations.

Of course, that's not the case for everyone. In my own life, my grandfather worked his whole career as a welder at Westinghouse, up in Lester, Pennsylvania. He lived about five minutes away from work. My grandfather started there at 23-years-old and worked until he was 65, putting in 42 years of dedicated hard work. Believe me, welding is not easy. It's a demanding job physically and mentally.

He retired at 65 and died at age 67.

How long did his retirement nest egg have to last? Two years. Planning in that scenario is easy – spend half the first year, then half the second year, and you'll be fine.

Kidding aside, situations like my grandfather's are more the exception than the norm. Today, my team regularly sees people who are 58 years old and want to retire at 60. They've had enough. The stress is too much, and they want out of the rat race. So, we start by doing the simple math. If you retire at 60, you may live into your mid-90s. In other words, you may be retired longer than you worked. So, is your retirement plan built to last 30 or 35 years?

In addition to the time span your plan must cover, is it able to handle the effects of inflation? You must include inflation into the mix or your plan will fail 100% of the time. Let's say you want to retire at age

60 and live on $5,000 per month in retirement. At just 3% inflation, by the time you're 84-years-old, which isn't particularly old today, that same lifestyle will cost $10,000 per month.

So I ask again, is your retirement plan built to last into your mid-90s and is it protected from the impacts of inflation? When my team runs reports for people, we include a 3% rate of inflation on expenses and build the plan out to age 100. That way, we're planning for the inevitable cost increases that come with simply being alive to experience them. By planning to age 100, we cover life expectancy and then some.

People usually say, "Age 100? Lord, I hope I don't make it to 100!" We have a laugh. But then I say, "You won't say that when you're 99," and they always agree.

If after reading this chapter, you realize you're making any of these mistakes, consider contacting a retirement expert. If you realize you're making them all, put the book down immediately and call an expert.

In all seriousness, these are only some of the more common mistakes I see. Like we discussed in Chapter Two, we're on a long journey and there are countless pitfalls that could arise. It's why you need a financial Sherpa guide.

This is especially true with Social Security, which we'll discuss in the next chapter. The right claiming strategy can mean thousands more over time. Conversely, claiming Social Security as soon as it's available or without regard to your other assets can leave hard-earned money on the table forever.

Chapter Four

Social Security

Back in the 1930's, President Franklin D. Roosevelt made a promise to America. No, it wasn't a chicken in every pot. President Herbert Hoover actually said that, though Roosevelt "borrowed" it.

No, President Roosevelt's promise was that beneficiaries of his Social Security program would never be taxed on their benefits. And he kept his promise – he never taxed it. Social Security benefits were tax-free from their inception in 1935 and remained that way for nearly 50 years.

But that party was too good to last. After decades of non-taxation, in 1983 President Ronald Reagan made Social Security benefits taxable.

Tax on your Social Security benefit is based on your "provisional income." That includes any adjusted gross income, tax-free interest, and half of your Social Security benefit. Once people hit a certain level of income, their Social Security benefits are taxed. As you can probably guess, Social Security taxes have only grown over time.

Year	Filing Status	Provisional Income Threshold	Amount of Benefit Taxed
1935	Single	N/A	0%
	Married	N/A	0%
1983	Single	$25,000	50%
	Married	$32,000	50%
1993	Single	$34,000	85%
	Married	$44,000	85%
Source: U.S. Social Security Administration			

In 1983, a single person was taxed on 50% of their Social Security benefit if their provisional income was $25,000 or more. For a married couple, it was 50% on their benefits if they made $32,000 or more.

A decade later, President Bill Clinton introduced the Congressional Re-Allocation Program. That policy's acronym is CRAP, and the content isn't much different. CRAP made the Social Security tax rate even greater and it's where we stand today. Single filers making $34,000 or more will have 85% of their Social Security benefits taxed. For married couples, it's $44,000 or more of combined income when the 85% level takes hold.

While it's not particularly desirable, to reduce the tax on your Social Security benefit, you must reduce your income. But that doesn't mean living off of less and less in retirement. Your income can remain the same, but you can legally tell Uncle Sam about less of it through "tax avoidance." That isn't to be confused with tax evasion. The difference is about 20 years in prison!

When we meet with people, we ask them to bring several documents with them, one of which is their tax return. We use that to see how much unearned income you're reporting. That means interest, dividends, and capital gains.

In today's interest rate environment, we don't see much of that on the typical tax return. Even if you had $1 million in the bank, the interest earnings would be paltry. Do we see capital gains? We're starting to, which is good because this bull market is more than a decade old. For years, we saw losses, specifically of $3,000. Why that amount? Because after you offset losses against gains, $3,000 is the maximum carryforward amount that losses can reduce ordinary income.

We do, however, see a lot of dividends on people's tax returns. People like owning stocks that pay dividends. They buy DuPont, Exxon, Aqua America, and other dividend-paying stocks. We may see $10,000 in dividends on the tax return. If so, my next question would be – what did you do with that money last year? Did you go on a cruise? Buy groceries? Pay bills? Everyone says the same thing – "We didn't get that money, it all gets reinvested to buy more shares. We don't even see that money."

In other words, people in this scenario pay tax on money that never makes it to their wallet. It's mind-boggling and all too common. To make a point, let's understand that the dividend yield on the S&P 500 is around 1.3%. What if I could find you a financial vehicle in a tax-deferred account that pays 2.5%? You would double your return, but it wouldn't be reported on your Form 1040 until you withdrew the money and spent it.

In this scenario, the $10,000 is not on the tax return, which reduces your adjusted gross income and the taxes you pay. It's also possible to reduce your Social Security taxes, so this strategy simply makes sense.

This strategy of reducing Social Security taxes worked a lot better 20 years ago. Was it because that was when Social Security started being taxed? No, that was 35 years ago. Was it President Clinton's tax hike? No, that more than 25 years ago. Those combined income thresholds – do you think they've ever been adjusted for inflation? Not once since 1983. What other government figures do not get adjusted for inflation? I can't think of many. The way I see it, this is a tax increase on senior citizens every single year.

But we keep hearing there is minimal inflation. Or that when there is clear inflation, it's just temporary. It will pass.

If you think about it, the government has an incentive to say there's little inflation. Otherwise, it needs to give Social Security beneficiaries a raise through a cost of living adjustment (COLA). There should be one every year, right? I mean, inflation in 2021 is running between 5-6%.

On top of that, when you turn 72-years old, you're forced to take money out of certain retirement accounts. They're called "required minimum distributions," or RMDs, and they only increase with age. As a result, the government is forcing your income up. And since the provisional income thresholds have never increased, that amounts to an annual tax hike.

If you take nothing more from this book, at least understand that income levels for Social Security taxes have never increased. You should be upset about that, which hopefully will lead to calls to your senators and representatives. Tell them to adjust the provisional income levels up for inflation. I wouldn't expect much though, and I'm speaking from experience. After all, why would the government want to enact changes that mean less tax revenue?

We've talked a lot about Social Security taxes, but not much about the actual benefits themselves yet. Your Social Security benefit is based on your highest 35 years of reported income. If you only worked 30 years, the government puts zeroes in for the last five and calculates the benefit. And while there are benefits available for the disabled and survivors, we're focusing on retirement benefits for the purpose of this chapter.

Did you know, there can be up to 567 ways for a couple to claim Social Security retirement benefits? Beyond claiming, which in itself is complex, there's also taxation and other considerations. So as you can see, this is an incredibly complex topic – consulting an expert would be wise.

In my opinion, if you're not coordinating when you claim your Social Security benefit within the overall framework of a retirement income plan, you're doing yourself a huge disservice. That's because coordinating Social Security with your other assets can lead to a much higher lifetime benefit.

For example, let's say you were 62 years old and had a monthly income need of $1,500. Many people will default to claiming Social Security to meet that income need. However, if you have other assets in play, it makes sense to consider the income need in the context of those other assets.

A monthly stipend of $1,500 is an annual pay-out of $18,000. If you had a sizeable Traditional IRA or 401(k) balance, say $500,000, why not take that $18,000 per year from there? That way you can wait on claiming Social Security and experience a greater benefit every year you defer. Plus, those gains are locked in for life. People don't understand how good of a deal that is. And without expert guidance, it probably wouldn't occur to you.

Now, besides qualifying for benefits, the first step to receiving them is claiming them. Let's start from the top – Americans can claim Social Security benefits beginning at 62-years-old. Claiming then is called "filing early." Full retirement age is 66 if you were born in 1954 or earlier. For those born from 1955-59, full retirement age scales incrementally until it hits age 67 for those born in 1960. That's where it stands now, until the full retirement age is raised again. It will happen because it's one of the remedies for Social Security's solvency concerns.

When you claim relative to your full retirement age determines your benefit amount. And in the simplest terms, it pays to wait, though not past age 70. You earn credits for each month past full retirement age that you delay claiming. The table below illustrates how lucrative it is to put off claiming Social Security. The example uses a full monthly retirement benefit of $2,000 for someone born in 1960 or later.

Age at Retirement	Monthly Benefit	Full Retirement (%)	Total benefit* ($)
62	$1,400	70.00%	$638,400
63	$1,500	75.00%	$666,000
64	$1,600	80.00%	$691,200
65	$1,734	86.70%	$728,280
66	$1,866	93.30%	$761,328
67	$2,000	100.00%	$792,000
68	$2,160	108.00%	$829,440
69	$2,320	116.00%	$863,040
70	$2,480	124.00%	$892,800

To age 100, does not account for inflation or taxes
Source: *U.S. Social Security Administration*

A word of caution is to be mindful of future benefit projections on your Social Security statement. They assume you'll be paying into the system at your last reported income until you file. That income level will likely be high and perhaps not in line with reality, which makes projections big. That could throw your retirement off course if you don't actually receive that much income. It's in the fine print on the statement and many people don't understand the calculation. Keep it in mind while planning your Social Security claiming strategy.

The truly essential question is *when* to claim Social Security. Well, it depends. First you have to answer one thing – when exactly will you die? If you can tell me that, I can pinpoint the time to maximize your benefit. Now, obviously we don't know when the end will come, so to prepare, we have to take several things into account.

First is your family history. What is the average lifespan of your family, especially parents and siblings? What is your personal health history? If you have health issues and nobody in your family makes it that long, you should probably take Social Security early. If you're healthy and have "good genes," you should probably wait.

But it's not just about you. If you're married, you have to factor survivor benefits into the decision. If one spouse dies, the survivor will get the higher of the two amounts. If the husband is the big breadwinner and the wife isn't, *when* the husband claims will have a direct impact on what the wife gets when he passes away. Of course, I'm assuming he passes first because women tend to live longer than men.

It doesn't stop there though. All in all, there are five key areas that need to be addressed to properly determine when to file for Social Security:

1. Health status
2. Life expectancy
3. Income needs
4. Whether you plan to work or not
5. Survivor needs

Unfortunately, most people claim early simply because they can. They'll say "you never know" to justify it, but that's shortsighted. They end up working well past age 62, but only until they make the maximum amount of annual income before Social Security benefits are docked. That amount, which is subject to inflation, is now around $19,000. For every $2 made above the cap, $1 of your Social Security is taken away. Of course, if you're still working, why take Social Security in the first place?

As we know, claiming early will cost you compared to waiting until full retirement age or beyond. There are a lot of reasons to defer Social Security. The primary reason is you get more money. If you want guaranteed income, Social Security is a guaranteed income source that you can't outlive, plus it's inflation adjusted. That is not typical of many income sources today. Some annuities can be structured similarly; however, they're not backed by the federal government. And don't forget – you've already paid into Social Security.

When it comes to spousal benefits, there are many rules to know. But I can give you a basic primer. To start, a spouse is entitled to half of the other spouse's benefit amount (the primary worker's benefit), if claimed at full retirement age. To collect a spousal Social Security benefit, the primary worker has to have filed. The spouse must be at least age 62 for a reduced benefit or full retirement age for a full benefit. Also, there are no delayed credits for spousal benefits past full retirement age. These are all important factors to know when planning, and something a retirement expert will impress on you.

Strategies to maximize Social Security for married couples have dwindled over the years because of legislation. Today, the only real strategy left is the restricted application, but the availability and advantage are dwindling. It's only available to those who turned 62 before Jan. 1, 2016. In 2024, those folks will be age 70, and the restricted application will be gone entirely.

There are several rules involved with a restricted application, and it can get complicated. But in essence, the strategy lets one person in a married couple file for a benefit on their spouse's work record. The other spouse must have filed already for this to work.

To give an example, say Jim is age 70 and his wife Nancy is 66. Nancy can file a restricted application for half of Jim's age 66 benefit, rather than her own. So let's say Jim collects $2,600 per month in Social Security at age 66. Nancy's restricted application can result in $1,300 per month for her.

Now, perhaps Nancy's own benefit is $1,800 per month. But instead of taking that, she'll take half of her husband's benefit and allow hers to grow until she's age 70. When she's 70, she'll switch to her benefit, which will be much higher than at age 66. In this instance, Nancy could receive $64,000 of income over four years while allowing her Social Security benefit to grow. People like when we can find them an "extra" $64,000 and guarantee 32% more in Social Security.

If you file for benefits before full retirement age or fall outside the restricted application eligibility criteria, you're subject to the "deemed filing rule." It says that when people file, they are filing for their greatest benefit available at the time. So if a spouse went to file at age 64 and said they wanted a restricted application for half of their spouse's benefit, they would receive the higher of their own benefit or their spouse's benefit. Thus, a restricted application isn't allowed to be filed until full retirement age.

If it isn't clear yet, spousal benefits for Social Security are not easy – and we've barely scratched the surface. It gets even more complex when talking about ex-spouses. But we can really help divorcees when they're planning for retirement. Most don't know they can collect on an ex-spouse.

To collect a Social Security benefit based on an ex-spouse's work record, you must have been married for 10 or more years. The ex-spouse must be 62 years old or older and, if the divorce was more than two years ago, doesn't need to have filed for benefits themselves. Lastly, the person receiving the divorced spouse's benefit must be unmarried. If all of these conditions are met, ex-spouses are entitled to half of the other person's total benefit. If they remarry, ex-spouse benefits end.

I had a client who was a nurse over at Children's Hospital in Philadelphia. She was divorced, 67-years-old, and never remarried. She came in and I asked for her Social Security estimate. She told me she wanted to wait to file until age 70 to maximize her benefit, which was smart on her part.

Then I asked why she wasn't collecting Social Security based on her ex-husband's work record. Well, she had no idea it was possible, that's why. They were married for more than 10 years, so she was entitled to half the amount of her ex-husband's benefit. No matter what the divorce decree states, federal law says your Social Security rights can't be bartered away. He wouldn't lose any of his benefit and would not be notified she filed. She still didn't believe me.

We talked more, and since her ex was a chemist and likely maximized Social Security, I told her it was possible she could be receiving $1,300 per month. She'd have to prove the marriage and divorce, but she was entitled to a benefit. The next day, she filed for ex-spouse benefits and started getting $1,300 monthly checks soon thereafter.

She came back a year later and was beside herself with joy. She was set to maximize her Social Security benefit by waiting to file until age 70. On top of that, because of our talk, she was receiving $1,300 per month. And that would continue until age 70. It amounted to $48,000 of income she never knew she had.

It gets even more complex with multiple divorces. But it's possible for more than one ex-spouse to collect on one worker, as long as they all meet the eligibility criteria. And believe it or not, the current spouse can collect on that person too. We hear of some famous examples, like the late Johnny Carson, who had three ex-wives collecting on his Social Security benefit.

If you thought Social Security benefits for ex-spouses was complex, survivor benefits are even trickier. I won't dive into the regulatory specifics. But if we were having a meeting in my office, we would get much more detailed. Instead, I'll provide the basics.

To receive survivor benefits, a couple must have been married at least nine months, except in the case of an accident. The survivor must be 60 years old or older to receive a partial benefit (50 if they're disabled) and full retirement age to receive a full benefit. The benefit is not available if a widow(er) remarries before age 60 (or 50 for a disabled survivor), unless that marriage ends. And finally, if the marriage lasted 10 years or more, a divorced spouse is eligible for survivor benefits.

Partial benefits and delayed credits can play a role in survivor benefits as well. Let's say a married couple, Mark and Kathy, are nearing retirement. Mark is 66 years old and Kathy just turned 60. They both still work, so neither has filed for Social Security.

If Mark unexpectedly passes away, Kathy would receive Social Security survivor benefits equivalent to if he had filed at age 66. If he were 69 years old and the same scenario unfolded, Kathy would receive benefits as if Mark had filed at age 69. In other words, delayed filing credits apply to survivor benefits. But, if a survivor benefit is claimed prior to full retirement age, it will be a partial amount based on several factors.

I can't stress enough how complex this issue is. There are so many ins and outs, that, if you're unaware of them, you could leave a lot on the table. It's exactly why you need an expert guide in retirement. I've consistently been able to find money for people, even after they've filed for benefits.

I want to conclude this chapter by providing this caveat: these are just a few considerations for Social Security. The right solution is highly personalized to your situation. As such, it takes a deep dive into the total picture and thorough examination of all the options to create a solid plan. Don't make the mistake of permanently leaving money on the table. Find yourself a Social Security expert, preferably before you file, but even if you're already collecting. It could make a world of difference.

Chapter Five

No Pension? You and Uncle Sam Could Be "Good" Friends

Even though some of us may stop working entirely in retirement, we don't stop paying income taxes. Our tax burdens could be smaller while retired – I say *could* be smaller – but the tax man still visits. And for many of us, it's because we have so much built up in tax-deferred accounts.

As we know, pensions are all but gone from the modern American benefit package. Those who still have them experience reduced payments or lump sum buyouts. Now more than ever, it's on us as individuals to provide for ourselves in retirement. So, we save, and with the help of our employer matches, we save some more.

Much, if not all, of this saving happens in "qualified" plans. These are plans that qualify for favorable tax treatment, including deferral, for both sponsors and participants. Variations of qualified plans include the Traditional IRA, 401(k), 403(b), 457 and more. There are two main types of qualified plans: defined benefit plans and defined contribution plans.

A defined benefit plan is an arrangement where the plan sponsor (the employer) provides a defined benefit to plan participants. In other words, it's a pension. The benefit could be a monthly paycheck, health insurance or a combination of similar perks. Providing and guaranteeing these benefits has become overly difficult, hence the move away from pensions.

The other type of qualified plan is the defined contribution plan, which means the employer provides a contribution to plan participants. These plans are the overwhelming plan of choice for employers offering retirement savings options for employees. The contribution often comes in the form of a match to employee retirement plan contributions. Company managers like this arrangement because they're absolved of the risk and pressure of managing a pension fund. Smartly, firms prefer to supplement their workers' savings every pay period rather than collect, invest, and distribute that savings over time.

Admittedly, when pensions were the norm, retirement planning was much easier. Income, and many times health care, was guaranteed for retirees. Retirement was basically a question of when. That's unlike today, where we save in qualified accounts, hoping it's enough to last, all while worrying about our health care. And we don't really consider taxes until it's too late to do much about them.

As you probably know, there are several rules that pertain to qualified plans. Most of them are created by the government, and just like Social Security, it pays to know them. And if you don't know them, you will likely pay. I regularly see people make mistakes with qualified plans and their resulting taxation.

For instance, I see people build up substantial wealth in these qualified accounts. Don't get me wrong, that's tremendous. The more people save, the better they'll be in retirement. Plus, there's immediate tax savings through a lower taxable income.

But the mistake they make is when it comes time to distribute those accounts in the form of income. Remember the required minimum distributions (RMDs) we mentioned last chapter? If you don't plan for them, they can sting, particularly early in retirement. And of course, there are several rules. In this instance, it's absolutely true that what you don't know about RMDs can hurt you.

First Year Distribution – Lower Tax Bracket?

When you turn 72, the government says to you, "We let you set up this account years ago. We let you contribute money to this account and gave you a tax deduction for it. We let it grow tax-deferred for decades. Now we want some of your money."

In other words, you're required to withdraw money from many types of tax-deferred accounts. It's roughly 3.65% of the balance in year one, with amounts increasing slightly (but steadily) in the following years. On a balance of $1 million, that's $36,496 – no small sum. And thus, your retirement tax scenario is born.

As I mentioned earlier, without pensions in the mix, people can build substantial wealth inside qualified plans. It's not unusual to see balances of $250,000, $500,000 or more than $1 million. Your exact RMD amount is based on the IRS Uniform Lifetime Tables, which we'll discuss further in a bit.

When you need to start taking RMDs depends on when you turn 72 years old. This is important for tax purposes, because there are penalties for getting it wrong. Say Joe is nearing his RMD date and has an IRA. In his first year, he can defer the withdrawal until April 1 of the following year. So, if Joe is 72 on Sept. 3, 2021, he has until April 1, 2022, to take his 2021 RMD.

In most retirement planning scenarios where deferment is an option, the advice is usually to defer as long as possible. But that's not the case necessarily with RMDs. That's because for each year after your initial RMD, you're required to make the withdrawal in the calendar year (i.e., by Dec. 31). For Joe, if he waits until April 1, 2022, to take his 2021 RMD, he also must take his 2022 RMD in calendar year 2022. That could mean a double tax hit for Joe in 2022, which isn't the best thing for people on fixed incomes.

If Joe's Traditional IRA has a $100,000 balance, paying taxes on about $7,423 for two years' worth of RMDs may not be a big deal. But if the account has $1 million in it, his two-year RMD total would be north of $74,232. That will put him in a higher tax bracket, and that's not how retirement is supposed to go. If that were the case, it would probably be better for Joe to take the first RMD in 2021.

Now, employer-sponsored retirement plans, like 401(k) plans, go by their own rules. That means you have to check your plan documents, because they will dictate the RMD criteria. That said, many follow the same rules as Traditional IRAs. But not all of them do, so be sure to understand the RMD rules and how they'll affect your taxes.

If You Still Work, You Have Options

If you work, are you subject to RMDs? Yes…and no. It depends on the type of account.

If you have a Traditional IRA and are 72, there are no exceptions. You must take an RMD or be subject to a penalty. It doesn't matter if you're working 80 hours per week, if you're 72 and have a Traditional IRA balance, you'll have to take RMDs.

With a company plan like a 401(k) or 403(b), the rules are a little different. If you're still working for the company, *and* an active participant in the retirement plan, *and* own less than 5% of the company, you don't have to take an RMD.

In that scenario, you could be 75 years old and maximizing the plan by contributing $27,000 per year (the maximum allowed with a catch-up contribution in 2022). The account could have a bunch of money in it. But because you meet the conditions mentioned above, you would not have to take an RMD.

Additionally, if that plan allows, you may be allowed to roll in other IRAs. That would mean you could take money where you were subject to RMDs and place it in an account where you're free from RMD rules. With that setup, you wouldn't have to take RMDs from *any* account until you retire.

Properly Calculating Your RMD

Most people have multiple types of qualified plan accounts because they've rolled over funds from previous jobs. Here's the thing, if you have five different qualified plan accounts, you're subject to five different RMD requirements.

Each January, you should receive a 1099-R statement for each of your accounts in which you've taken a distribution. It will show how much money you've received so you can report it on your tax return. The custodian will also report to you what the fair market value of the plan was as of Dec. 31 of the previous year. Someone with five accounts would take all five fair market value forms and add up the plan balances. Their entire annual RMD amount will be based on the total of all five plan balances.

This method applies for qualified accounts. A Roth IRA is the only qualified account not subject to the RMD rules and can be excluded. Roth 401(k) accounts, on the other hand, are subject to RMD rules. These RMDs are a great reason to roll Roth 401(k) plans into a Roth IRA prior to age 72. Then you'll be able to avoid RMDs altogether on those assets.

Once you have your RMD total, refer to the Uniform Lifetime Table from the IRS that I mentioned earlier. It's Table III in IRS Publication 590-B. I have them all over my office – I keep a few in my briefcase too. They're available online at IRS.gov as well.

The table will give you the relevant divisor for your age to apply to your total qualified account balance and determine your RMD. For age 72, the current factor is 27.4. For a $1 million qualified account balance total, that means the first year RMD is $36,496, or roughly 3.65% of the balance. As you age, the divisor gets smaller, meaning the amount you're required to take out gets bigger. Make no mistake, the government wants your money.

Most people will use Table III of IRS Publication 590-B. That is the one used in the example above. However, if there is a 10-year or more age difference between married spouses, a different table is needed. That is Table II of IRS Publication 590-B. Thankfully, the government realizes the difference in ages and doesn't want the younger spouse to run out of money prematurely. So, there is a different divisor that allows for less to be withdrawn from the account annually.

There is a worksheet available as well from the IRS to help people correctly calculate their RMDs. This is something people should do every year so they know where they stand. But even if they do that, knowing the total RMD amount is only one piece of the puzzle. There are rules too about which accounts generate the distributions.

Take from the Correct Account(s)

This is probably the biggest mistake I see people make. Again, people today may have several different qualified accounts because of job changes. A 401(k) here, a 403(b) there, an IRA with rolled over funds someplace else – it can get messy over time.

Say Charlie comes into my office with $500,000 in a 401(k) and another $500,000 in a Traditional IRA. There's $1 million total in his portfolio. We know his first year RMD will be around $36,496.

Can Charlie take the RMD out of either account, or does he have to take it out of both?

In this case, he *must* take it out of both because they're different types of qualified accounts. That means he'd take $18,248.18 out of the 401(k) and $18,248.18 out of the Traditional IRA.

Compare his situation to Jennifer's scenario, who also has $1 million. But her nest egg is split in even $200,000 chunks across five different Traditional IRAs.

Can Jennifer take the RMD out of any one of the Traditional IRAs? Or does she have to take it out of all five?

She can take it out of one because they're all the same type of account.

Now, the rules can get convoluted here. You can combine Traditional IRAs and take it out of one. You can combine 403(b) accounts and take it out of one.

You can't combine 401(k) accounts. I've seen people with four 401(k) accounts from different employers. How many different distributions do they have to take? Four. You can't take the RMD out of just one account because you'll incur penalties on the other three.

Another thing to keep in mind is that IRAs are individual accounts. Even for married couples, the accounts are owned by an individual. That means accounts cannot be combined for distribution purposes and RMDs must be accounted for individually. A husband must take the proper RMD from his account(s), and a wife must do the same from hers.

Let's go back to Charlie, who has $500,000 in a 401(k) and $500,000 in an IRA. He must take half of his total RMD from each account – $18,248.18 from each. I've seen people take the entire $36,496 from one and call it a day. Their 401(k) is a dog, the options stink, while the Traditional IRA is doing well. So, they pull the entire RMD out of the 401(k) and move along. But, if Charlie did that, he would be subject to a penalty.

What's the Penalty?

I've mentioned penalties a couple times. Do this wrong, penalty. Do that incorrectly, another penalty. What exactly are the penalties? Well, they're not cheap. This is not your garden-variety 10% early withdrawal penalty.

This one is 50% – it's the real McCoy.

What does that mean for the person who takes an incorrect distribution, even if it was a mistake? In Charlie's $1 million case, he was supposed to take out $18,248.18 from the Traditional IRA. He instead took the full $36,496 from his 401(k). That would cost him 50% of the RMD he was supposed to take from the Traditional IRA, or $9,124!

That stinks. But it gets worse.

Charlie would have to write the check for $9,124 immediately to the government. On top of that, he's still on the hook for the $18,248.18 RMD. What's that money subject to? Federal income tax.

He lost 50% of the RMD amount, then another 22% in taxes to the "corrected" RMD. And if he lives in a state that taxes retirement income, he'd lose even more.

What's left for Charlie?

That sound you hear? Oh, that's Charlie slipping and sliding down his personal Mount Everest. If he keeps it up, he will run out of money.

Charlie and people like him better know the rules or work with someone who does. Otherwise, it will be costly. And believe me, there are a ton of Charlies out there – I see it all the time.

Buck Tradition, Go Roth

You may remember me mentioning that Roth IRA accounts are free from the RMD equation. Because of that and a few other reasons, a Roth IRA is a great way to build wealth.

In 1997, the late Senator William V. Roth Jr. helped introduce a new IRA that would bear his name. Roth IRAs were part of the Taxpayer Relief Act of 1997, designed to help people save for retirement and more. They also can be used to purchase a primary residence, pay for medical expenses or fund a child's college education. Plus, Roth IRAs have no RMDs and growth is tax-free because they're funded with after-tax dollars.

Of course, that's all contingent on you waiting until age 59-and-a-half to withdraw any earnings. You can withdraw your contributions to the account at any time. But if you withdraw earnings early, you're looking at a 10% penalty, plus the money will be taxed as regular income. Additionally, these assets are subject to the five-year lookback rule, which we'll discuss in the next chapter. Even with all that said, Roth IRAs can be one of the best assets in a retirement portfolio, if you adhere to all of the rules.

To be frank, when I first heard of Roth IRAs, I thought our politicians had lost their marbles. I mean, the deal is almost too good to be true. Thankfully, they're still in place today, to the benefit of many savers.

I think a reason they're still in place today is because they haven't caught on. For some reason, the Roth IRA is not as prevalent as the smartphone. Pretty much everyone should have one, yet not everyone does. But I think I know why.

For many of us, the concept of delayed gratification is as mystical and unrealistic as a unicorn. We want everything now. Why wait? We want it NOW.

People will say, "but I might die tomorrow," and use that as justification for making short-sighted decisions. I counter that thinking with this – if you die tomorrow, and you're not broke today, you had enough money.

Tax break later (Roth IRA)? No, people want it today (Traditional IRA). It's the same concept we talked about last chapter in relation to Social Security.

And just like maximizing Social Security, Roth IRAs are primarily built on the concept of delayed gratification. You use dollars taxed at today's rates to benefit yourself years down the road. When you withdraw that money after age 59-and-a-half, you'll do it on your timeline and pay no taxes. That's a huge benefit, though it won't be experienced for many years, possibly.

Let me put it another way.

Say you entrusted someone with $10,000 to invest on your behalf and wanted the money back in 10 years. And let's say he or she performed a miracle for you and after a decade presented an account balance of $100,000.

Which would you rather pay the taxes on, the $10,000 or the $100,000? With a Roth IRA, you pay on the $10,000. With a Traditional IRA, you pay on the $100,000.

In this context, it's clear that a 10-year wait is too long for many people. It's also clear that Roth IRAs are great deals and probably should be a part of everyone's portfolios. That's not to say a Traditional IRA is bad. To be sure, both Traditional and Roth IRAs can successfully live in the same portfolio. Still, there are differences between the two types of accounts.

Roth IRA	Traditional IRA
After-tax contributions	Contributions are tax deductible immediately
Tax-free withdrawals	Withdrawals taxed
No RMDs	RMDs at 72
Access to principal	Penalties for early principal withdrawals

It is possible to convert a Traditional IRA to a Roth IRA. If you don't have a Roth IRA, or you have one along with a Traditional IRA, it could make sense to convert the Traditional IRA to a Roth. But there are many things to consider in the bigger picture beforehand.

For instance, your current income tax rate matters because that's what you'll be taxed to do the conversion. For the transaction to make sense, your current rate must be lower than your future projected rate in retirement. That is, the rate at which you would be taxed when withdrawing the money from the Traditional IRA. In other words, if your tax rate now is lower than you think it will be in retirement, it makes sense to pay today's lower rate rather than the higher rate in the future.

To give an idea of the income tax implications, say you're working and so is your spouse. Together, you're bringing in $125,000. If you decide to convert a $100,000 Traditional IRA, you'll be taxed on $225,000 of income the year you convert. Let's also say that neither of you have pensions and you want to live on $50,000 per year in retirement. Given that, it probably doesn't make sense to do a Roth conversion while you're working.

The fact is, you have the most tax flexibility after you retire. Remember, most people don't use what the government gives them. We pass out tax charts to people in our office so they understand where the tax bracket lines fall.

Do you know how much a married couple can make and remain in the 12% tax bracket? At today's rates, it's about $83,000. When you add in the standard tax deduction, the 12% bracket ceiling rises to about $108,000.

If you want to live on $50,000 per year in retirement, you still have $58,000 of income available in your tax bracket, if needed. So, you could do a $58,000 Roth conversion and pay just 12% in taxes on it. This strategy follows the advice I give to clients, which is to fill up your tax bracket, because most people don't. Absent expert help, you probably wouldn't capture such an opportunity. My point is, use what the government gives you.

Another important consideration for a potential Roth conversion is your withdrawal horizon. When you're doing a Roth conversion, what's the potential downside? The taxes on the amount that is converted. That's why people don't do it – the fear of a big tax hit.

The reason to do the conversion, the tax-free growth and withdrawals, are what can compensate for the upfront tax hit. But it all has to make sense, and that comes down to the timeline. To determine whether the tax implications are worth it, you have to look at when you'll experience the tax-free benefits of a Roth IRA.

Will that happen immediately? No. It could take six-to-eight years, or maybe even more. If you need income from the account immediately or within six-to-eight years, a conversion may not make sense.

A final consideration for a Roth conversion is how you'll pay the conversion tax. If you need to pay the conversion tax out of the Roth IRA you just converted, it probably doesn't make sense.

Let's say you had a $100,000 Roth IRA and wanted to convert it. It wouldn't make sense to pull $30,000 out of the converted account to pay the government.

But if you had that $30,000 you'll owe the government in a taxable account elsewhere, it could make sense. For instance, if it was in a mutual fund account, with the S&P 500 at or near all-time highs, it might make sense. Or if it was in a brokerage account with our bullish market, it might make sense. Or maybe you even have $30,000 sitting in your sock drawer. Regardless, if you have the funds, you can use that money to pay the Roth conversion tax. That will give you $100,000 in a tax-free retirement account for the rest of your life.

If one of your legacy goals is to pass money down, Roth IRAs are fantastic. You can leave a legacy and experience minimal tax interference. The 2019 Setting Every Community Up for Retirement Enhancement (SECURE) Act eliminated the possibility to "stretch" the benefits over a beneficiary's lifetime. However, beneficiaries still have a full decade to liquidate the account.

As you can see, qualified plan taxation can be eerily similar to a slippery slope on a steep mountain. But with proper care, you can navigate the terrain to maximum advantage. It's definitely an advantage of having an expert guide!

Chapter Six

Your Chances of Needing Long-Term Care Are Either 0% or 100%

Let me preface this by saying that long-term care is a highly complex and detailed topic. This chapter is not meant to be a comprehensive source on the subject. Rather, it's meant to educate and provoke further thought and action.

Believe me, there's a clear need for a chapter like this. That's because when you say the phrase "long-term care" to most people, their first thought is usually, "it won't happen to me." When we leave a nursing home for the first time as a visitor, we almost all think the same thing – I'll never let that happen to me.

And that's one of the biggest myths out there – people think they're safe from rather common health ailments. The numbers tell a different story.

Lifetime Possibility from Age 65 On		
Major Life Event	For Men	For Women
House Fire	2.20%	2.80%
Severe Car Accident	15.50%	18.00%
Disability or Cognitive Impairment	44.00%	72.00%
Source: American Association for Long-Term Care Insurance, 2021		

While awful to experience, a house fire is a relatively unlikely occurrence for people age 65 and up. Even a severe car accident, which we may think is a 50/50 proposition, isn't nearly that likely.

However, Americans age 65 and up have about a 68% chance of becoming disabled or cognitively impaired in their lifetimes, per the Family Caregiver Alliance. That means being unable to do basic daily things like groom, eat, or walk.

For men, it's a nearly 50% chance. Unfortunately for women, it's a more than 70% chance of disability or cognitive impairment. Now, I'm no doctor, but I'm fairly certain that women fare worse because they're driven nuts by us men.

Seriously though, you can say it will never happen to you. But what if it does? Who will take care of you?

This is an important financial *and* health-related consideration. You can go broke paying for health care. And as we'll see, that's an actual strategy for some. But for my clients and me personally, being covered financially and medically is vital.

Of course, there's Medicare. And until it's officially declared to be done and dusted, we can continue to rely on it. But in a disability or cognitive impairment scenario, you may not be "sick" under Medicare's rules. Sure, you can't walk, bathe, or remember much, but you won't qualify for coverage under Medicare.

On top of that, consider Fidelity's 2021 Retiree Health Care Cost Estimate. It says the average American couple needs $300,000 for health care while retired. A 2017 study from PWC says a couple needs $172,000 for long-term care. And that doesn't include costs for over-the-counter medications and most dental services, which can add up.

We're talking about almost $500,000. Is your portfolio built for that?

Of course, an option is to ask your family – that's free, after all. But isn't that simply a shift in cost? Your family will have to give up time and perhaps even income to care for you. Plus, there will be more costs – you'll need medical equipment, medicine and more. And what will happen to the family dynamic? I've seen it get ugly when the stress of caretaking adds up.

Undoubtedly, health care in retirement is expensive (another reason it pays to be healthy). It takes an emotional toll too, which has a cost of its own, even if not in actual dollars and cents.

My team and I see it all the time. A health concern springs up, the bills roll in, and the stress levels rise. If the family is serving as caretaker, it can be even worse as medical costs and stress from providing care compound each other. Within that context, let's look at an all-too-common health problem – Alzheimer's disease.

Lifetime Risk for Alzheimer's by Age and Sex		
	Men	Women
Age 45	10.30%	19.50%
Age 65	11.60%	21.10%
Source: 2021 Alzheimer's Disease Facts and Figures (Alzheimer's Association)		

Almost everyone I speak with knows someone who has been affected by Alzheimer's disease. In fact, my grandmother died because of the disease.

Now, as we know, we're living longer collectively. So, here's a scary statistic – according to the same data from the above table, 43% of people age 85 and up are afflicted by Alzheimer's disease.

Nearly half.

So, in essence, if you live long enough, there's an almost 50/50 chance you'll be stricken with Alzheimer's disease.

Understanding that, there are some troublesome, but vital, questions to ask. In particular, how will you pay for care in retirement, especially late in life?

There are four basic ways to cover these needs:

1. Long-term care insurance
2. Pay your own way
3. Government aid
4. Care communities

Long-term care insurance is not that popular among my clients and others I speak with regularly. When I ask why, they often cite cost.

I get that. But when you have other insurances that are too expensive, like your auto and home coverage, what do you do? Raise the deductible. By doing that, you absorb more risk and the insurance company takes on less. As a result, you're charged less in premium.

If you can do that with home and auto insurance, why not with long-term care? You can. In fact, tell the insurance company or broker what you're willing to spend. Say, "I have $300 per month, that's it," or whatever the number may be, and go from there. It won't cover everything, but it will allow you to formulate a plan for long-term care. And in my opinion, covering something is better than covering nothing.

The other argument I hear against long-term care insurance is whether nursing home care will be needed or not. This is why I say your chances are either 0% or 100% - you either need it or you don't.

To relieve that concern for people, there are solutions called "hybrid plans." That's a combination of long-term care insurance and life insurance. So you'll either use it for care, or your family will have a tax-free benefit. Either way, you're not throwing the money away.

The second way to cover care in retirement is self-insuring everything – also known as **paying your own way**. I often hear people say that they're definitely not going to end up in a nursing home – but – if they do, it doesn't matter because they're rich. They'll pay out-of-pocket.

Fair enough. Nursing homes today cost a lot. Are you prepared for that?

What's a lot?

The 2020 Genworth Cost of Care Study says it's anywhere from about $93,000-105,000 per year, depending on accommodations. Another study, the 2010 Employee Benefit Research Institute's report, "Effects of Nursing Home Stays on Household Port-folios," says the average stay in a nursing home is 299 days. Of course, that's just the average.

The same study notes that 10-20% of nursing home residents have been there for five or more years. But some conditions, like Alzheimer's disease, mean patients can be in a home for a decade or more.

If you do the math, it adds up to a lot of money. For an average stay of 299 days at the low end of the nursing home cost scale, you're looking at more than $67,000. If you had Alzheimer's disease and were in a home for six years, it's closer to $500,000. Footing the bill yourself, you could conceivably spend your entire nest egg on medical care.

Of course, you could simply **let the government pay for it by using Medicaid**. The government pays for everything anyway, right? Go on Medicaid.

It's a great program – except for one thing. It has a very high deductible. How high? Pretty much everything you own.

You don't go on Medicaid until you're out of money. A married couple on Medicaid is allowed to keep a house and a car – perhaps $120,000 in total assets. Whatever is owned above that value would need to be sold and used for medical care.

What happens to a married couple though, ultimately? One of them passes away. Then they're not a married couple, but an individual. And a single person on Medicaid is allowed to have just $2,000 to their name.

If you're an individual and you own a house? List it. A car? Sell it. Any other valuable assets? Sell them all and take the proceeds to pay the nursing home until you're down to $2,000 in total assets. Then you'll qualify for Medicaid.

Oh, and there's a five-year lookback period. That means any asset transfers within five years of the Medicaid application could be subject to penalties.

When you apply, the government will ask for five years of bank statements. They want to see when money left the account and where it went. You truly are required to spend your assets on medical care to qualify for Medicaid. And if you lie, it's perjury. So, you'll go to jail instead of a nursing home.

Someone using this strategy needs to realize two things. First, they must spend their assets down to basically nothing to qualify, or have the ownership transferred. And second, it has to be done at least five years in advance of the Medicaid application to avoid penalties.

To give an example, a client came in one day concerned about her father. He was 84 years old, had about $500,000 in assets, and lived in a nearby assisted living facility. It cost $5,500 per month, but he had an old long-term care policy that paid $6,000 per month for life. That's a great deal, and he should be set. My client was relieved.

But what if dad took a turn for the worse and needed full-time nursing care? What do things look like then, especially for the $500,000 in assets? That's when the situation got a bit more complicated.

My client called and found out the rate for full-time nursing care – $12,000 per month. That's another $6,500 per month, or $78,000 per year, needed for care. At that rate, he'll go through the $500,000 quickly once taxes and other costs are included.

Figuring that dad would trend towards full-time care next as opposed to leaving assisted living altogether, it was time to act. We needed to get the $500,000 in assets out of his name as soon as possible. That way, the money can stay in the family instead of going to pay for care with the intent of eventually qualifying for Medicaid.

So, we cashed everything out. We paid tax on some things and some surrender charges, but in the end, we liquidated everything. It all happened with a documented paper trail and was put into the daughter's name.

In the end, my client's dad ended up making a sizeable monetary gift to his daughter. Was it all $500,000? No. But what was the alternative? He goes in to nursing care and loses the money to the care facility. Instead, we started the five-year clock. The best-case scenario is dad stays in the system for five years and applies for Medicaid. When the government asks if he made any gifts in the last five years the answer will be "no." Then, the family assets are safe.

What if he gets sick in three years? Then he'd have to pay the additional $6,500 per month for two years, which is $156,000 total. Losing $156,000 is better than losing $500,000, right? After he paid for two years, he'd apply for Medicaid. Once again, any gifts in the last five years? No, because we started the clock ticking at the right time.

In summary, it's possible to play that game with Medicaid. If you want to avoid penalties, get all assets out of the applicant's name. Again, if it's a single parent and they have a house, sell it or put it in a child's name. The key is to <u>document every transaction meticulously</u>. The onus is on you to prove everything.

The last way to pay for care late in retirement is to **live in a "care community."** I'm sure there are some near where you live. They're billed as wonderlands for seniors, with everything they'd ever need – from food to recreation to health care. And that's what they are for the most part. They're beautiful facilities with a lot to offer. There certainly are places like that in my neck of the woods.

And they're all free, right? Not at all. Far from it. You have to buy that housing unit in the community. How much is that? It could be from $100,000 to $1 million, according to AARP. Depending on the part of the country, it varies. Around me, they can be $200,000 to $400,000.

Is that the only cost? No. There's also a hefty monthly fee on top of the cost to literally get in the door. And there could be more in addition. But, if you can afford it, living in a care community can be a terrific option for retirees.

Generally speaking, that's about it when it comes to the basic choices for funding care in retirement. Either buy long-term care insurance, pay entirely out of your own pocket, do the Medicaid spenddown, or buy into a care community.

Now, the good news is that most people plan on living a long time. However, the bad news is that most people don't have a plan for doing that.

If you plan on living a long time and think, "It won't happen to me," let me ask you something. How many people thought it would happen to their 94-year-old parent? Did your friends think it would happen to theirs? Did either of you think you'd have to take care of your parents? Probably not. So, it's wise to plan for what will likely be a difficult situation for your family.

In my family, we didn't plan for my mother to get lung cancer – it was an enormous surprise for us all.

She'd always been pretty healthy. In fact, she had just come back from Florida and passed a physical. When she went to the doctor for her next checkup, a small thing turned into big deal.

During the exam, she reminded the doctor about a persistent cough she'd had since before the trip down south. He ordered a chest X-ray to dig a little deeper.

Soon thereafter, we found out she had lung cancer. The bloodwork leading up to the X-ray was fine and nothing else looked abnormal. Still, cancer. Talk about the unexpected.

The diagnosis was she had a tumor and it needed to be removed. That was done, followed by rounds of chemotherapy and radiation. At the end of all that, her total hospital bill (before insurance coverage) was in excess of $1 million. That's a hefty tab for an unexpected incident.

All that was quite an ordeal for my mother and our family, but it's good that we planned. We had coverage in place, so while the situation wasn't on our radar, we were ready for the financial side of it.

Now fast forward to this year and she needs two knee replacements. So when do you have the bulk of your health care? If my mother's experience is any indicator, it's late in life. We're able to live longer, and that comes with a cost.

The point is, you never know what you may have to go through. Take my mother's example. Her need for long-term care went from nothing to 100% in the matter of a few doctor visits. The same can happen to anyone. Get help and make sure to plan accordingly.

Chapter Seven

The Last Leg of The Retirement Relay Race

To me, retirement planning is a four-leg relay race. The first two-and-a-half legs or so are about saving and investing. I'm talking about retirement savings, home(s), cars, education and possibly more, depending on the situation.

Generally, you want to spend less than you make, save regularly and progressively with income increases, and be smart about debt. On the last point, I mean use debt to your advantage, not to fund designer clothing or travel. And that's the first couple legs of the race in a nutshell.

This time is when we should all be stuffing money away for retirement. I like to joke that you should start thinking about retirement very early in life – like when you're born. Like a business, you should think about the exit plan when you're starting up.

But in reality, it should start with your first job. Whether that's your first newspaper route or first job out of school is up to you. The earlier, the better.

That's because the most important dollar in your retirement plan is the first one. The dollar you cram in on catch-up savings right before retirement might be worth $1.10 in retirement. The dollar saved at age 18 or 21 could be worth $15+ when you hang up your boots.

Once you start, it's then about saving continually, no matter what. In other words, pay yourself first and don't deviate. If you started in your twenties, you'd have a lot of those "$15 singles" when you retired. That's the magic of compound interest.

Albert Einstein said, "Compound interest is the eighth wonder of the world. He who understands it, earns it. He who doesn't, pays it." Compound interest is interest upon interest on top of the initial investment (or debt). For savers, it's the steadiest, most surefire way to wealth.

For those who start saving for retirement early, time is an ally because there's more opportunity for compounding and recovering from downturns. Those who start late often view time as an enemy because they wish they had more of it.

Either way, it's important to build that foundation of personal savings during the first couple legs of the race. As we know, today the onus is on us to fund our retirements. And it's important to have a base because there are some potentially big retirement blind spots out there.

For instance, your expenses will almost always rise to the level of your income. I've also heard it referred to as "lifestyle creep." It basically means many people will eventually start spending what they earn (or more).

Think about it, you get a raise or a bonus, and you instantly think about that new car, trip or whatever it is. Maybe you eat out more often. Maybe it's first-class only when flying now. Whatever it is, your expenses will almost always rise to meet your income.

Another blind spot is not accounting for emergencies, even in retirement. You need an emergency fund because emergencies happen. It's as simple as that. If you plan for them, they're not emergencies. Your car will break down. Your furnace will die. And let's be honest, these emergencies never stop, no matter your age.

According to a 2015 report from The Federal Reserve, 47% of Americans wouldn't be able to cover an unexpected $400 expense without borrowing money or selling something they own. In other words, nearly half of the country is living on an incredibly thin financial line.

Perhaps people get in that situation because they can't distinguish between needs and wants. That's another blind spot I see often. We think we need to have a daily cup of gourmet coffee, or, on a larger scale, those designer clothes, or the fancy car.

But, all that stuff drains our assets and income to the point where we "can't afford" a required $400 brake fix on the car. Such behavior will erode a retirement nest egg, or more likely, prevent one from being established altogether. That's why people don't have enough for retirement – they blow their money while working.

Believe it or not, you can "live without" easier than you think. Years ago, my wife Cindy and I were in a different spot in life. To be frank, we were living "bare bones." We were in a spot that an unexpected $400 expense would've hurt.

Of course, one night our dishwasher stopped working. What did we do? We went without and washed dishes by hand. It was kind of fun. She washed, I dried. We spent time together washing dishes and bonding. We liked it so much, we didn't get a dishwasher for two years!

It comes down to what's a want and what's a necessity. You don't need a dishwasher. Are they nice to have? Absolutely. Over time, our situation improved, and we eventually decided a dishwasher would be helpful. But those two years without a dishwasher prove it's possible to live without.

That said, you don't need to live a Spartan existence. We don't work so hard to deprive ourselves of joys. Some people want nice toys, gadgets or whatever, and that's perfectly fine. But keep things in perspective. Don't let your desires overtake your budget and your retirement plan. Ask yourself, and answer truthfully, what is a want, and what is a need?

Doing that on a regular basis will help you avoid yet another blind spot – comparing yourself with others financially. We also call it "keeping up with the Joneses." It leads to pouring ridiculous amounts of money into things like throw rugs, decorative grass and more, all in the name of trying to impress others.

When it's time to retire and you you're not able to, you'll rue those purchases. That's because what's right for you and your family could be different than what's right for others. Before trying to keep up with other people, walk at least a mile in their shoes. Then you'll know what they're going through – and it will likely change your perspective.

Job loss is a hugely damaging blind spot, particularly when it's close to retirement. Nobody ever sees it coming, but it happens every day.

A couple who had become clients a few weeks prior came into my office for a consultation. During our first meeting, they told me about the security of each of their jobs. He was with DuPont in a managerial role and had been there for years. He was 62 years old and wanted to work until age 66, but his company was (and is) in flux. Several changes, including mass labor force downsizing, continue to occur. So, they were rightfully unsure about his prospects.

The wife was about the same age as her husband and wanted to work a few more years before retiring. She was employed with a local company that owned several restaurant franchises. She was part of the back-office staff that handled business matters for all the franchises. The family-owned company was always good to her, and given the nature of her work, they were confident she'd have the job for a while.

Flash forward about a month and they're back in my office to sign contracts. The topic of their jobs comes up again.

Guess who was let go? The wife.

Some members of the family who owned the company decided to sell their stakes and retire. Thus, she and others were no longer needed because there would be no more business matters to handle.

The couple never saw it coming. It's the quintessential example of how job loss is a big blind spot. I believe that The Lord provides. But it can be stressful to get through these situations. The point is, you never know what can happen, so it pays to be prepared.

One more common blind spot is the effect of your family on your retirement. By that I mean, the costs you endure because of family matters like a sick child or parent. Let's be honest, who plans for their kids or parents to get sick? It's understandable that this is a blind spot.

Still, it can be damaging financially and otherwise. I've had people in my office that stopped working at age 61 to care for a sick parent. That's at least a few years of potentially foregone saving and company matches, which would help in retirement. Plus, the emotional toll of providing care causes stress and other complications, as we spoke about in the last chapter. The solutions to these situations are seldom easy. But, even if you had to prematurely retire, sound planning can mitigate the damage.

Now, you would think bad market conditions, bubbles and crashes would be on the radars of those near retirement. But they're not, which makes adverse market conditions a blind spot for people. How many people lost their jobs because of the 2008-09 crash and never saw it coming? In the end, economic conditions dictate a lot of things, including payroll budgets.

The other market-related blind spot I see a lot is the false belief that what happened yesterday will happen today. It's called "recency bias" and has caused many retirement plans to falter. I saw it in 2001-02 and again in 2008-09. People think they'll earn 10% annually forever and act as such. But when the return is paltry or negative, they don't adjust their withdrawal. They think they'll be fine and do nothing. Well, enough down years without withdrawal adjustments and the possibility of going broke looms large.

That's where guaranteed income comes in, to provide a steady stream of money to cover regular expenses. It's so important to have guaranteed income now that we don't have pensions. However, a blind spot is people relying *solely* on a guaranteed income stream. That leaves them without an emergency fund. I hate to break it to you, but your roof doesn't care if you're retired, it still needs repairs every so often.

If your only income source covers expenses like housing, food, health care and such, there's little room for financial emergencies. Things are going to happen

– your furnace will break, cars need repairs, and so on. Even if you're retired, you need money set off to the side for emergencies that isn't part of the guaranteed income.

Let's say your budget in retirement is $5,000 per month. Does that include $24,000 for the new roof you need? That's another $2,000 a month for a year, and it's not in the budget if you rely on a solitary guaranteed income stream.

Some people plan for these kinds of big expenses before retirement. I call them the smart ones. They will get the new roof, furnace, vehicle or whatever done before they retire, whether it's an emergency or not. The advantage is they're still working, earning, and saving, so it's easier to pay for the $24,000 roof. What I see a lot is a couple will be near retirement and their roof is 20 years old. They know they'll need a new one, so they get it done before retiring. They do the same thing with housing, windows, HVAC, vehicles, and other big-ticket items.

The people who don't plan find themselves retired and in need of a new driveway or something like that and, unfortunately, it's not in their budget. So, what do they do? They take out a home equity line of credit (HELOC) and finance the purchases through debt. Luckily for them, it hasn't been a big hit because interest rates have been low for years. But if and when rates rise, the HELOC won't be as attractive an option.

The real damage of this blind spot is when people are near or in retirement, and they have both a mortgage *and* a HELOC. If not managed carefully, that situation could lead to debt payments for life. And those payments become even more expensive when rates rise. I doubt that's how most folks envision retirement.

A way to alleviate almost all the blind spots we just talked about is to save early and safe often for retirement. Saving is so important because, later in life, we need that base of assets to draw from. Without it, retirement is merely a dream. Pensions are gone and in the last leg of the race, we don't have the luxury of time on our side.

So, saving is important, all throughout life really. But a big thing to keep in mind when saving is inflation and how it affects your savings. This is particularly important in the last leg of the race.

Say Jim and Carla are married, each is 55 years old, and they're nearing retirement. They each want to work until age 66 and think $5,000 per month to live off would be great. The problem is, they're thinking in today's dollars. When we factor in a 3% inflation rate, which is a bit more than the historical average, they'll need $6,400 per month for the same lifestyle at age 66.

It gets worse with time. Generally, prices double every 20 years because of inflation. Think about how much milk, gas, cable TV and more cost now versus in 1997. Thus, the person with a fixed $5,000 per month for life in retirement will be able to buy less over time.

The key here is that you have to factor inflation into the equation, and too many people fail to do it. The last legs of the race are about preserving assets – keeping what's yours – and inflation is part of that. The only tried-and-true method I know to offset inflation is to save more. It sounds simple, and that's because it is simple. If you have more income available, you're able to handle price increases.

When you're approaching retirement, or "in the last leg of the race," it's the right time to remove yourself from exposure to market risk. That means moving investments away from equities and towards safer vehicles. This quote captures the sentiment well:

The prudent see danger and take refuge, but the simple keep going and pay the penalty.

Proverbs 22:3

The problem is, many people aren't equipped to make these and other investment decisions. It's why Target Date funds are so popular. It's as close to "set it and forget it" as you can get with retirement investing. You pick an end date (retirement) and the fund adjusts over time to more conservative investments.

That approach is better than the other one I see a lot, which is to look at past performance and pick the winners. It's another example of recency bias, and it's like locking the gate after the dog ran away. Not only are you chasing past performance, but it will probably stay that way.

See, the problem is people set their investment allocations and basically forget about them. Absent the management of the Target Date fund, people often remain too aggressively invested risk-wise for their ages. As they near or even enter retirement, they're exposed to way too much risk.

And if you end up on the wrong side of a market downturn because your assets aren't protected, it can kill your retirement before it starts. A sequence of consecutive returns around retirement age, good or bad, can affect your long-term prospects severely. The key period is about three years before retirement and five years afterwards. The potential for negative returns is why we call this concept the "sequence of returns risk."

Say it's 2000 and Fred is ready to retire. His nest egg is $750,000 and he wants to draw $45,000 per year to live, which is 6% of his total assets.

Let's assume he wants to invest in mutual funds but keep it simple. So, Fred puts the money in an S&P 500 Index Fund, which generally did great in the late 1990's. He heard it held a broad range of companies and had done well in the past. Given his retirement goal, let's see how that would have unfolded.

Year	S&P 500 Return
1997	33.36%
1998	28.58%
1999	21.04%

Retire in 2000				
Year	Balance	Income Distribution	Investment Gain/Loss	End Balance
2000	$750,000	$45,000	-9.11%	$640,775
2001	$640,775	$45,000	-11.88%	$524,997
2002	$524,997	$45,000	-22.10%	$373,918

Sources: S&P 500 historical data, Dan White and Associates

Without question, the consecutive returns early in retirement (the "sequence of returns") devastated Fred's portfolio. Because of severe market dips, the principal was cut by nearly half.

In 2000, Fred went through 14.6% of his nest egg in 12 months. The next year, because he was still in the S&P 500 fund and drew the usual amount, his balance was about $525,000. So, in two years, Fred lost 30% of his portfolio because of his exposure to market risk.

At that point, Fred would likely wonder how long he could stay retired. Regrettably, he stayed in the S&P 500 fund and maintained his $45,000 draw. And by 2002, nearly half of his nest egg was gone because of a sequence of poor returns.

Fred's fate was avoidable.

For instance, he could've left the S&P 500 fund and invested in cash, a laddered series of bonds or a fixed-index annuity. These vehicles could have protected him from risk and may have increased in value, or at least lost less than the S&P 500 Index.

Unfortunately for Fred, different timing alone could have saved his portfolio. Retiring three years earlier with the same nest egg would've meant three straight years of growth to begin retirement. Even if he remained in the S&P 500 fund the entire time, the difference in retirement dates is enormous:

Retire in 1997				
Year	Balance	Income Distribution	Investment Gain/Loss	End Balance
1997	$750,000	$45,000	33.36%	$940,188
1998	$940,188	$45,000	28.58%	$1,151,033
1999	$1,151,033	$45,000	21.04%	$1,338,742
2000	$1,338,742	$45,000	-9.11%	$1,175,882
2001	$1,175,882	$45,000	-11.88%	$996,533
2002	$996,533	$45,000	-22.10%	$741,244
Sources: S&P 500 historical data, Dan White and Associates, LLC				

Retire in 2000				
Year	Balance	Income Distribution	Investment Gain/Loss	End Balance
2000	$750,000	$45,000	-9.11%	$640,775
2001	$640,775	$45,000	-11.88%	$524,997
2002	$524,997	$45,000	-22.10%	$373,918
Cost of Poor Timing (Retiring in 2000 vs. 1997)				-$367,326
Sources: S&P 500 historical data, Dan White and Associates, LLC				

Without foresight and action to remove themselves from risk, Fred and people like him must find work. Or they'll need to greatly reduce their standards of living shortly after retiring.

Here's another example. Say you put $100,000 in a retirement account and are withdrawing $5,000 per year, beginning in 2000. The money is invested in an S&P 500 index fund.

How long will the money last?

Well again, because you're starting in 2000, you lose 45% right out of the gate in the first few years. You'd probably call your broker, who would tell you to hang in there, it'll come back.

Five years later, you've got about half your original account balance back. But then in 2008, you lose half again in the market crash, leaving you with just under $30,000.

In this case, the answer to the question is the money would last less than 17 years, running out in 2017. You wouldn't even get your $100,000 principal back. You'd only get about $85,000.

Year	No Principal Protection	
	S&P 500 (%)	$100,000
2000	-10.14%	$85,367
2001	-13.04%	$69,887
2002	-23.37%	$49,723
2003	26.38%	$56,521
2004	8.99%	$56,153
2005	3.00%	$52,687
2006	13.62%	$54,182
2007	3.53%	$50,918
2008	-38.49%	$28,244
2009	23.45%	$28,695
2010	12.78%	$26,723
2011	0.00%	$21,723
2012	13.41%	$18,966
2013	29.60%	$18,100
2014	11.39%	$14,592
2015	-0.73%	$9,522
2016	9.54%	$4,954
2017	19.42%	$0
2018	-6.24%	$0
2019	28.88%	$0

Sources: S&P 500 historical data, Dan White and Associates, LLC

Now take the same scenario and reverse the returns of the S&P 500 over the past 20 years. So, the down years of 2000-2002 would be the last three years instead of the first three.

Year	No Principal Protection	
	S&P 500 (%)	$100,000
2019	28.88%	122,436
2018	-6.24%	110,108
2017	19.42%	125,520
2016	9.54%	132,018
2015	-0.73%	126,090
2014	11.39%	134,883
2013	29.60%	168,328
2012	13.41%	185,230
2011	0.00%	180,230
2010	12.78%	197,624
2009	23.45%	237,795
2008	-38.49%	143,192
2007	3.53%	143,070
2006	13.62%	156,875
2005	3.00%	156,432
2004	8.99%	165,045
2003	26.38%	202,265
2002	-23.37%	151,164
2001	-13.04%	127,105
2000	-10.14%	109,723

Sources: S&P 500 historical data, Dan White and Associates, LLC

In this scenario, you'd have $110,000 left *after* withdrawing $100,000 over a 20-year period.

What's the moral of the story? What are we told? Buy low and sell high. Where are we? With markets seemingly near all-time highs on a regular basis. If I were within a year or two of retirement and had all my money in the stock market, not preparing for sequence of returns risk would keep me up at night.

When you combine what we just discussed with the earlier points about expenses and debt in retirement, the whole picture starts to become clearer. Hopefully at this point, you're able to see the difference between thinking in terms of assets versus thinking in terms of income. It's not how big your nest egg is in retirement, but how much you have to live on each month.

Put another way, would you rather have $1 million or $6,000 per month for life that adjusts with inflation? Most people would take the latter. In the end, it comes down to guaranteed income.

Much of what I do centers on getting guaranteed income[1] for people, mostly because they don't have pensions anymore. Or, if they do, it's a reduced payout. Either way, as in the example above, people prefer the security of a guaranteed monthly check over an asset balance. I help them get there, many times using annuities.

The term "annuity" sparks doubt, suspicion, anxiety and more in some people. They know the stories of friends and family being sold a garbage annuity from a slick advisor who won't return phone calls now. Their

---

[1] Annuity guarantees are based solely on the claims paying ability of the issuing company and compliance with product terms.

contract is muddled with language they don't understand, it's expensive and restrictive. I hear this a lot.

However, the right annuities can be a great fit in in the last leg of the race. An annuity is basically an income stream for life. Guess what else are income streams for life? Social Security and pension programs. If they're fine in most people's minds, the right annuity should be too.

Three main types of annuities exist today, and we could write a book on each one because of their complexity. To provide a brief summary, this table highlights annuities and their features.

Type of Annuity	Features
Fixed	• Safe from market risk • Can track an index for growth potential • Tax-deferred
Variable	• Acts like mutual fund (has subaccounts) • Potentially high fees and risk • Tax-deferred
Immediate	• Turn cash into an income stream • Cash refund or return of principal • Live long enough, get paid beyond principal

Annuities do have complications, such as potentially high fees for early withdrawals. Plus, the documentation can be a burden. It's another reason to have an expert guide helping you. He or she can make sense of everything, because in the end, you need to know what you're buying.

Even with their intricacies, annuities provide what people really want in retirement – peace of mind. That's what you should aim for when you create your retirement income plan. This is the blueprint for the last leg of the retirement journey, and annuities can certainly be a part of the strategy. In fact, they probably should be if you don't have a pension.

You need an income plan because in retirement, you switch fully from saving mode (accumulation) to protection and spending mode (preservation). And that can be tough because we're conditioned to save. But the spending is on your life – housing, health care, hobbies, travel and so on. And without a job and steady paycheck, or a much smaller one than usual, it takes a plan to have the income you'll need in retirement.

Here's an example of a retirement income plan. It assumes other potential blind spots and leaks, like long-term care and such, are covered.

The primary purposes of this income plan are to provide guaranteed income, protect the asset base, and allow for some market growth. This could be for a married couple on the verge of retirement. The plan emphasizes a hybrid approach of "buckets" and an "income floor." The "buckets" hold assets and are designed based on when the assets will be needed. The "income floor" is a minimum level of guaranteed income.

Say Mary Ann and Bob have $500,000 in assets and need $30,000 per year, adjusted for inflation, to live. Their assets would form the base of a personal pension plan. Now, the income floor may not cover all of their expenses, but it will help. So, let's also assume they receive $1,000 per month from Social Security too, covering the income gap.

The first bucket would harvest income, with minimal exposure to the market. The main aim is for this bucket is to be accessible and safe because it's for near-term expenses.

Bucket 1 (Years 1-5): $200,000	
Equities	10%
U.S. Bonds *(1-3-5 year ladder)*	45%
Cash, CDs	45%
Goals: Liquidity, Protection	

Since Bucket 2 isn't needed for six years, there can be a bit more exposure to the market. In addition, this bucket would house a fixed-index annuity, ideally purchased at least five years earlier. Mary Ann and Bob would defer payments on the annuity so it could accumulate value. When it's needed, the payments can be turned on for guaranteed income. Bucket 2 would have a 3-5-10 year bond ladder, which when combined with the other assets, will provide more guaranteed income.

Bucket 2 (Years 6-10): $150,000	
Equities	30%
U.S. Bonds *(3-5-10 year ladder)*	35%
Fixed Index Annuity 1	35%
Goals: Modest Growth, Some Liquidity, Protection	

We can take on more risk in Bucket 3 since the assets won't be needed for more than 10 years. That said, this bucket needs to provide guaranteed income later in retirement. So it can't be too tied to the potential tribulations of the market. As a result, a sound mix for this bucket would include another deferred annuity and diversified stocks, bonds, and CDs.

Bucket 3 (Years 10+): $150,000	
Equities	50%
U.S. bonds *(3-5-10 year ladder)*	25%
Fixed Index Annuity 2	25%
Goals: Semi-Aggressive Growth, Protection	

The income floor is built in the plan in a few different ways:

Income Floor (Years 1-10+)	
Years 1-5	Cash, CDs
Years 6-10	Fixed Index Annuity 1
Years 10+	Fixed Index Annuity 1 & 2
Goals: Protection, Guaranteed Income	

In total, this approach creates an income floor and uses other sources to fill the gaps. Protecting Mary

Ann and Bob's assets is crucial, and by limiting market exposure, income is ensured. But there's some leeway built in so they can experience gains if the market is good.

We've spent a lot of time on the last leg of the retirement race. But we've really just begun. To illustrate the point a final time, let me paint two pictures for you.

One is of a couple, both age 93, who owned a business. They benefited from this business their entire working lives. Money was never an issue, as their lifestyle reflected. They sold their stake for $1 million 35 years ago. Thinking they'd live until their 80's, they're running low on money in their 90's.

The other picture is of another married couple, also age 93, both of whom were grade school teachers. Neither ever made more than $65,000 per year. However, they retired at age 60 with pensions. Each gets $4,000 per month guaranteed for life and have been for nearly 35 years.

Which picture would you prefer?

Every income situation is unique, and it takes time to understand the whole picture to plan accordingly. I know this is a lot to cover. But when you're talking about retirement income, the lifeblood of successful golden years, it's important to make sure things are being done right.

Chapter Eight

Avoiding Estate Planning Nightmares

For many people, leaving a legacy is an important part of the financial planning process. But a true estate plan is more than simply naming beneficiaries. It's comprehensive and has wide-ranging ramifications. That said, there are really only two main reasons to create an estate plan:

1. Directing assets after you die
2. Sidestepping big estate taxes

Without a doubt, everyone should have an estate plan in place, no matter their net worth. However, few do. I would estimate that 75-80% of the people I meet do not have an estate plan. To give you an idea of what I mean by "estate planning," here are some common documents in an estate plan and a bit about each.

Will		
Purpose	***The Good***	***The Bad***
Directs assets	Controls legacy	No tax planning
Names guardians	Protects wealth	Uncontrolled assets

Living Will		
Purpose	***The Good***	***The Bad***
Provides terminal illness care wishes	Respects your wishes	Can be obsolete if not updated

Healthcare Proxy		
Purpose	***The Good***	***The Bad***
Authorizes a care agent	Trusted advocate(s)	Can be obsolete if not updated

Power of Attorney		
Purpose	***The Good***	***The Bad***
Authorizes a financial agent	Trusted advocate(s)	Can be obsolete if not updated

Trust		
Purpose	***The Good***	***The Bad***
Directs assets	Controls legacy	Costly
Eases tax burden	Protects wealth	Buyer's remorse if irrevocable

Creating a plan that fits with your situation means working with a financial advisor and an attorney. That's because what you don't know about estate planning can hurt you. So, it's best to work with experts. I'm not an attorney and don't create these documents, but I've sat in several meetings with clients' attorneys.

Together, we help make sure your wishes are reflected in every aspect of your health and finances.

To me, estate planning is every bit as important as the rest of your retirement plan. It answers the question of where your money will go. But, if you're like many people, you have a minimal estate plan that's outdated, or none at all. It's not for a lack of wanting, though – almost everyone in this position has been meaning to fix it for a while, sometimes even decades. I get it, we procrastinate because we don't want to plan for our own death. But believe me, you're better off having a plan in place than leaving your estate unprotected.

A will is the simplest estate planning document out there, and something that people have or intend to create. Why? They want to avoid probate. But a will doesn't do that. In fact, a will pretty much ensures your estate goes through probate. The whole point of probate is to prove one's will.

So, when you're not around, your will is examined in probate court. That means your inheritors will hire attorneys, pay court fees and so on. In Pennsylvania, where I live, estate attorneys can charge up to 6% of the gross value of the estate. On a $1 million estate, that's a cool $60,000 – you don't have to do too many of those to earn a living.

And the costs associated with probate are just the start. The entire process can be lengthy. Examining the estate and settling any debts associated with it can take years. When there is real estate involved, it can get especially messy because all debts have to be settled before any distributions from the estate can take place.

That means the house may have to be sold. But while that's happening, there are still utility bills, tax bills and more associated with the house. All of those have to be settled too. The entire process can take months or years, which can be really tough for families.

So how do you avoid probate?

One way to avoid probate is to title every asset joint with rites of survivorship for the husband and wife. Assets will then pass to the surviving spouse. But the problem is, when one spouse dies, there's one left. So, when the last spouse passes the assets through a will, the estate is going through probate. The probate process in this scenario isn't avoided, but delayed.

A better approach is to use beneficiaries because assets passed this way avoid probate court. So, your retirement accounts, annuities and life insurance policies will not go through probate if your beneficiaries are accurately set up.

Any other financial assets that don't have beneficiaries, and there are a lot of them – brokerage accounts, CDs, mutual funds, bank accounts and more – can still avoid probate. For those assets, contact the financial institution and set up a "Transfer on Death" (TOD) or "Payable on Death" arrangement. This can remove most, or all, of your financial assets from probate.

Even with financial assets out of the probate mix, that still leaves real estate. How can you pass the house down to your loved ones and avoid probate?

People think they'll put it in their kids' names. That can work. But it can get messed up quick if you and the kids aren't on good terms. That big fight at Christmas could lead to an eviction. And what if your child gets a divorce? Your ex-in-law could kick you out. Or imagine if your child was in a car crash and got sued by the other driver. The house could be lost to a legal judgement.

Lastly, if the unthinkable happens and your child predeceases you, unless they changed their estate documents to leave you your home, you're out. And even if they did change their documents, you'll have to go through probate to get your own house back. So, while titling in your kids' names can work, it can also be ripe with pitfalls.

A better solution to avoiding probate with real estate is a revocable living trust. This document is like a will. But, with a will, the assets are titled in your name. If they don't pass by beneficiary, they pass through the terms of the will, which means probate and all its time and fees. With a revocable living trust, the assets are titled in the name of the trust, which offers several benefits.

I have a revocable living trust – The White Family Revocable Living Trust. The trustees are my wife and me. Anything we put in the trust, we control. So, all our assets that don't pass by beneficiary are titled in the name of the trust, not an individual.

That means property we own is titled in the name of the trust. Our mutual funds, bank accounts and brokerage accounts are all there too. But the assets that pass through beneficiary – the retirement accounts, life insurance policies and annuities – remain in the name of an individual and don't have to be retitled.

As a trustee, I still get the tax bills for the properties and pay all the associated fees for the assets. But, when my wife and I pass away, the state will ask, "what did Cindy and Dan own?" The answer is nothing. We didn't own anything. The White Family Revocable Living Trust owns it all, and the trust is alive and well. The trustees, unfortunately, are not. Thus, the successor trustees – my kids – would oversee the trust.

Now, my kids could go to a financial institution where I have an account and explain that their parents are gone. They'd have to show the death certificates and trust documents to prove they're the beneficiaries. Once they did, they could request an immediate check because they're the rightful beneficiaries to the account.

In this scenario, there's no court, no attorneys, no fees or time delay for my kids – just their rightful assets, in full. A quicker path to peace of mind is one of the best reasons to create an estate plan. In this example, it literally paid to work proactively with an attorney and financial advisor to create an estate plan at a cost of a few thousand dollars. The alternative is to have your family go through probate at a cost of maybe tens of thousands of dollars, or more.

Trusts offer a lot more options beyond real estate protection. However, that's a topic for another book entirely. The point is that you should know about trusts and what they can do for your assets. People think they're fine with a will, when that's really over-looking what else is available from an estate planning perspective.

Another key piece of an estate plan that is over-looked is the durable power of attorney document. It allows a person of your choosing to handle specific health, legal and financial obligations on your behalf, should you ever be unable to act yourself.

When is it needed? Well, frankly it's needed when the stroke, car crash or heart attack you had didn't kill you. Instead, it left you paralyzed on your right side, unable to do many things, like brush your teeth, eat, and sign documents. Thus, you need an advocate. And that's exactly what you'll get with a durable power of attorney – an advocate of your choosing.

People think they don't need a durable power of attorney because their beneficiaries are all set. Well if they die from the stroke they had, then that's true. But let's say you had a stroke, didn't die and your spouse now must care for you. That's not easy or cheap. If your spouse is the beneficiary on your financial accounts – which are individual, not joint – all that means is they get the assets when you die.

But you're not dead.

So, by relying on your beneficiaries being set and thinking all is well, you've put your spouse in an awkward position. That is, your spouse may possibly want you dead because that's how to get the money.

Or, in a less gruesome example, say the market is tanking. Your spouse may want to make investment changes in retirement accounts to protect assets. Without a durable power of attorney, that would not be possible.

In lieu of a durable power of attorney, your spouse would have to apply for guardianship. That can take weeks or more and cost a lot. In one case, I saw a guardianship agreement cost $15,000. A durable power of attorney is usually a few hundred dollars at most. It's better to have one and never need it than to need one and not have it.

Going back to beneficiaries for a bit, the example I gave earlier about my kids being beneficiaries to a retirement account was straightforward. That's because the beneficiaries were set up correctly.

The simple and key advice here is always name a beneficiary on accounts where you're able to, and keep them up-to-date. If you don't do that, it will hurt your retirement because, if your beneficiaries aren't set up correctly, it can be a nightmare.

For the vast majority of people I see, retirement accounts are their biggest assets. And these assets won't pass on through a will or trust. They pass on by beneficiary. Now, the account holder may have filled out that beneficiary form 30 or more years ago. Think it's reflective of their life today? I doubt it. There could be kids and grandkids now, or perhaps a divorce – either scenario would likely change the beneficiaries you would want for your accounts.

When selecting beneficiaries, you'll need to select both primary and contingent ones for your accounts. It's important to name both, and usually people do by naming their spouse as primary and any children as contingent. But if there is no contingent beneficiary named and the primary one is already dead, the entire account is going to probate. Name beneficiaries on these accounts and keep them up to date.

If you don't, you could end up like Bruce Friedman of New York. His wife Anne was an educator since the age of 23. They were married for nearly 20 years. During that time, Bruce would see Anne's retirement statements and just assumed he was the beneficiary.

One day, Anne had a sudden heart attack that took her life. Obviously, Bruce was devastated. His life was torn apart.

Well, it got worse when he went to claim Anne's $1 million retirement account as a beneficiary. It turns out, Anne did name beneficiaries. Pension officials found a form she filed 27 years prior when she got the job. At that time, she was unmarried and would not meet Bruce for another four years. The form officials found listed her mother, uncle, and sister as beneficiaries on her pension account. That meant Bruce was not the beneficiary as he thought.

Anne's mother and uncle had passed away already, but her sister Virginia was still alive. She collected the money and gave Bruce nothing, which is her legal right because of the beneficiary designation.

I don't imagine Anne wanted it that way. But, I don't have to imagine, and neither do any attorneys or anyone else, because there is a clear designation on the beneficiary form. It may not be the one Bruce wants, but it's legal nonetheless. The moral of the story is obvious – keep your beneficiaries up to date!

Besides keeping beneficiaries updated, also set up your contingent beneficiaries on a "per stirpes" basis, if possible. "Per stirpes" is a Latin phrase and literally means "by branch." For beneficiaries, it means the designation extends down the bloodline to include a beneficiary's spouse and children.

Say a couple had three children, all of whom are now adults, each with families of their own. Each of the couple's children is listed as a beneficiary on the couple's retirement accounts. This designation was made nearly 30 years ago, when the kids were small and the account just started.

Under such a beneficiary scenario, if one of the adult children had passed away, the couple's assets would be directed to the other two adult children. That sounds fine on the surface, but now the deceased child's surviving family is cut out of the picture. That's probably not what the couple would wish on their grandkids.

To avoid this scenario, set up a per stirpes distribution. That way, the deceased child's surviving family would be included as a beneficiary on the couple's account.

Now, you may say this seems like an uncommon occurrence. And yes, maybe it is. But you know what? It happened to me.

As I mentioned, my father died when I was 21 years old. Since he wasn't that old when he passed, his mother (my grandmother) was still alive, as were his brothers (my uncles). A few years after my dad passed, his older brother passed away. And a few years after that, my grandmother passed away. At that point, only his little brother was left of my dad's family.

My grandmother didn't have much, but she did leave some inheritance behind. But since her beneficiaries were not set up on a per stirpes basis, my uncle was the sole beneficiary because he was the only named beneficiary still alive.

As a result, my family and some of my extended family received nothing from my grandmother's estate. Is that what she wanted? Probably not, but we'll never know. It doesn't mean she didn't love us or anything like that. I just don't think she knew. Do yourself a favor and avoid this situation by setting up your contingent beneficiaries on a per stirpes basis.

Another beneficiary-related strategy I want to mention centers on whether to take a lump sum payment for a pension or not. You might think this topic is more appropriate for the chapter on income planning. However, I want to highlight a specific estate planning angle to the decision.

Most people want the security of the pension. And I get it, it's guaranteed income. Say a retiree has the option of a $600,000 lump sum payout, or a pension with a guaranteed income stream of $3,000 per month. If the retiree dies, their surviving spouse gets $1,500 per month.

Like I said, most people want the pension. But if both the pensioner and spouse die on the way home from the retirement party, those pension assets are gone and can't be passed to your kids.

Conversely, if they take the lump sum payout, they then have to manage it. And if they run out, it's gone.

I see this situation a lot and almost always advise to take the lump sum payout and purchase an annuity that is a better fit than the pension. It's the personal pension plan design we discussed in the last chapter.

Part of the better fit is the annuity's stability relative to the pension. Some pensioners in my area are unsure if their companies can honor their pensions. An annuity is backed by an insurance company, which also needs to be researched, but the best ones are built to last.[2]

---

[2] Annuity guarantees are based solely on the claims paying ability of the issuing company and compliance with product terms.

The other major piece in terms of fit is an annuity's survivor benefits versus the pension. An annuity's assets can be passed intact to beneficiaries. Once a pensioner dies, that's it, there is no more money. Most retirees I talk with want to leave a legacy. With a pension, that can be tough.

These considerations are worth keeping in mind, even if you're already receiving pension checks. That's because some pensions are offering lump sum payouts to those who've already begun receiving benefits. You never know, you may receive the call one day.

Admittedly, we've covered a lot. With so many rules and details, this topic is undeniably complex. And it really should be considered in the bigger picture of your entire life – both health and wealth. That is exactly why you should work with an estate planning attorney and financial professional. Together, they can craft a plan that honors your wishes and protects your assets.

Chapter Nine

The Cost of Procrastination

Many people in the medical field will say that hypertension, or high blood pressure, is the silent killer. Symptoms can go undetected for years until the damage eventually becomes evident.

We in the financial field point to other "silent killers." Many, myself included, feel tax increases are a silent killer. This is especially true of clandestine increases, like the lack of a COLA for Social Security beneficiaries we discussed in Chapter Four.

But the other silent killer, one that we can all directly control, is procrastination. You know, putting things off until tomorrow...only "tomorrow" doesn't seem to ever arrive.

Procrastination rears its head all throughout retirement. It can start early – like putting off saving when you first start working. And it can show up late too – how old is that will again?

Below is a hypothetical example of the power of two incredible forces – procrastination and compound interest. The following tables show the fates of four individuals – Fred, Betty, Wilma, and Barney. The example assumes a 12% average annual return because back in their time, (pre)historical returns were excellent. As you'll see, each person is a saver in their own way, and time can be both a friend and a foe.

The first table is for Fred. He's a hard-working guy who loves his family and having fun. Overall, he's decent with his finances and has steady, reliable income. He's close to retirement and wants to hang up his boots at 65-years-old, but he didn't start saving until age 35.

Fred		
Age	Savings	Balance
22-34	$-	$-
35	$4,459	$4,994
45	$4,459	$103,151
55	$4,459	$408,010
65	$-	$1,349,863

At this rate, he can retire at age 65 with more than $1 million by saving about $4,500 per year for about 30 years. That's $133,770 overall. It's no small chunk of change, but not something that will bankrupt his family.

Now Betty is someone who likes spending time with her family, and money when she's not with them. However, she's not a complete spendthrift. Her income is sporadic, but she is able to earn a good living. Still, she got a late jump on saving, not starting until age 45.

Betty		
Age	Savings	Balance
22-44	$-	$-
45	$14,937	$16,729
55	$14,937	$345,540
65	$-	$1,350,045

Betty wants to retire at age 65, but it will take a serious saving effort. For her to experience the same result as Fred, she'll have to save nearly $15,000 per year, or almost $300,000. That is a tall task, but it's not impossible. With Betty, we can see the cost of waiting.

Wilma, like Betty, enjoys spending money. But unlike Betty, she *is* a spendthrift. Wilma's credit cards are in frequent use and rotation. In fact, some of her epic daylong shopping trips resulted in smoldering plastic. She came late to the retirement saving party, not starting until age 55. Plus, while her income is steady, it's on the low end of the pay scale and always has been.

Wilma		
Age	**Savings**	**Balance**
22-54	$-	$-
55	$58,357	$65,360
65	$58,357	$1,349,980

As Wilma ages and her savings remain minimal, her time to save is running out. To experience Fred and Betty's desired nest eggs, Wilma will have to save almost $60,000 a year if she wants to retire at age 65. In that short saving period, she'll have to save $641,927! That's likely too tall a task for most people, perhaps even Wilma.

Last, and certainly not least, is Barney. Like Fred, he loves his family and a good time. Also like Fred, his income is steady and he wants to retire at age 65. Unlike Fred, Barney started socking money away early.

Barney		
Age	**Savings**	**Balance**
22-27	$2,000	$18,178
28-35	$-	$45,008
45	$-	$139,788
55	$-	$434,161
65	$-	$1,348,440

Clearly, Barney is the winner because it cost him just $12,000 to achieve a more than $1.3 million nest egg. Barney's example is an excellent snapshot of compound interest over a decades-long savings timeline. Simply put, if you save early on, you'll benefit much later in life.

While that example is hypothetical, it shows how time can be your friend, as with Barney and Fred. Or it can apply pressure, like it did for Wilma and Betty. That's what procrastination does. It applies unneeded pressure to a retirement plan. In the worst case, procrastination can make someone give up saving for retirement altogether because it seems pointless.

What's the cure?

Unfortunately, it's not as easy as just going to the doctor to get an anti-procrastination pill. But if you could, it would probably be to some kind of procrastination specialist.

Because when we have a health issue today, there's a specialist for it. Heart problem? Cardiologist. Foot problem? Podiatrist. Need a new hip or knee? Orthopedist. And so on.

No wonder we're living longer these days – because every time you have something wrong, you see a different doctor.

It makes sense though because medicine has become way more advanced and complex than 40-50 years ago. True, not many doctors make house calls like back then. And paying for health care is a lot more challenging in modern times. But then again, there were no robots performing surgeries 40-50 years ago.

In the same vein, do you think retirement planning has become more complex in the last 40-50 years?

You bet.

The problem with both our health and our finances is that we don't make time to see the specialists. We, well many men at least, tend to avoid doctor visits until it's medically required, the pain is unbearable, or both. And the Economic Policy Institute says nearly half of families in the U.S. have no retirement account savings at all. So, I'd say we aren't seeing our financial specialists enough either.

So let me ask you – when did you last take your retirement plan to a specialist? I am not a doctor. I am certain though that seeking help is the first step to curing financial procrastination.

Perhaps it would make sense to see someone who focuses on the "50 and up" crowd. Maybe someone who keeps up with every tax law change that comes down the pike and how it impacts you and your retirement income. Maybe somebody who keeps up with the thousands of retirement income products on the market to identify which ones will best meet your needs.

Maybe it's time you took your retirement plan to a specialist before it suffers another 2008 heart attack. Just the same, perhaps it's about time to see an expert who will also help get paperwork in order in case of a real heart attack.

That's one of the biggest signs of procrastination I see – estate planning documents, particularly durable powers of attorney. Sometimes people are put off by the cost of a will or trust. But, compared to what it provides, the cost of a couple hundred dollars at most makes durable powers of attorney worthwhile.

People think they're fine by naming beneficiaries alone. They figure that when they're dead, their beneficiaries will reap the rewards. And yes, that's true – when they're dead. But, what if they don't die?

Say tragedy struck. You were in a car crash and woke up in the hospital, paralyzed and barely conscious. With a durable power of attorney in place, your spouse can make health and financial decisions on your behalf. And usually, they're decisions you've actually made yourself earlier, your spouse is simply carrying them out. In the same situation without a durable power of attorney, your spouse is powerless.

Let's take another example – one I've seen happen in real life. Say a husband is in a coma resulting from a terrible car crash. His wife is at his bedside, hoping for a recovery. They don't have durable powers of attorney for each other. It's something they've been meaning to do, but haven't. Now she can't be an advocate for her husband. She can't make care decisions, nor can she make financials decisions. If he passes away, she is the beneficiary of his assets. But, he's alive, albeit in a coma.

If she needed access to his assets to pay for care, she's in a tough spot. She'll have to apply for guardianship, which we know can takes time and money.

Here's a side plot that can be devastating, though most people don't think about it. Say the above example plays out in 2008, during big market downswings.

Sure, money would likely be the farthest thing from the mind in such a context. But it still matters. If the husband is near retirement and still invested heavily in equities, he would be set for big losses at a bad time.

This situation is this – the market is tanking, he's in a coma, and his wife is powerless until she has guardianship. His assets are losing big value every day and they can't do anything about it. When the wife finally gains access to his accounts, they'll be down by a third or more. And that puts them in an even tougher spot because now there is less money for essential care.

It all could've been avoided with durable powers of attorney in place. But they procrastinated, and now they're in a tough situation without many options.

Sure, you can think bad things won't happen to you. But what if they do? People don't plan to get into car wrecks, but they happen. It's a part of life – not the good part, mind you – but a part of life nonetheless. So, you can wish and hope all you want that "life" doesn't happen to you.

<u>I can't say this clearly enough – hope is not a strategy.</u>

People come into our office for an initial meeting, and it usually lasts about 45 minutes or so. One of the last things we ask is for them to look five years into the future and describe their ideal financial situation and where they'd like to be.

Most people start their answer with, "I hope…" They *hope* the market remains strong. They *hope* it keeps going up. They *hope* it doesn't crash.

They hope hope hope, and then hope some more. Well, my clients don't want me to base their retirement income on hope. They'd prefer the bedrocks of their plans be guaranteed income[3] and predictable returns. As their advisor, so would I.

Below is one of my favorite biblical quotes. It's from the Book of Proverbs, which I read from each morning.

A wise man will hear and increase in learning, And a man of understanding will acquire wise counsel.

Proverbs 1:5

You're likely reading this book to increase your learning. And hopefully I've shared some ideas that have helped.

I firmly believe we should always continue to learn and improve ourselves. And yet, we'll never know as much about anything as someone who devotes their life to it. So, it also makes sense to seek expert help. And perhaps it's time to attain some wise counsel. Why wait any longer? Take your retirement plan to a specialist.

---

[3] Annuity guarantees are based solely on the claims paying ability of the issuing company and compliance with product terms.

If you work with an advisor already, that's great. It wouldn't hurt to get a second opinion. You'd do it for major health concerns. Why not for your retirement? It's not far behind on the list of what matters, at least it shouldn't be. And don't wait. We've seen how expensive that can be.

Chapter Ten

Save the Reservations for Restaurants

The focus of retirement planning really revolves around a key question – what are you trying to do with your money?

That question may seem simple on its face, but when you really think about it, the answer is complex. That's because it's based on your financial needs, values, vision and goals. Each of those can be quite complex on their own. Taken together, they provide a clear answer to what people are trying to do with their money.

When people come to my office, I ask them to bring their needs, values, vision, and goals. That is the truly important stuff, and the basis of their plan. Don't get me wrong, I also ask for their tax returns, account statements, and so on. But those are just pieces of paper with numbers on them.

I don't have minimum account size requirements or anything like that. When people who want retirement help come to me with their needs, values, vision and goals, I can help them.

It's done through a comprehensive process that results in sharing strategies, options and tactics to protect principal and guarantee income[4]. In other words, your money will be protected through future downturns. Plus, your income will be guaranteed, which is true no matter if you live to age 75 or 105. And it will be protected from inflation.

Sounds good, doesn't it? To me, retirement planning done right really means peace of mind. If you have a plan that covers everything you'll need in retirement, and is protected from market crashes and inflation, you'll sleep easy.

A successful retirement is possible, yet so many people have reservations about working with experts who can help them. Obviously, folks are entitled to their opinions. And believe me, I've heard thousands of them over the years. People have their reasons to not get expert help with retirement planning. Perhaps you do, even after reading this book.

But I don't buy into most of them.

For instance, when people say they have to "think about it," they're kidding themselves. They've likely been thinking about it for a long time and not acting.

If I've raised a question in your mind about what you're doing with your retirement planning, or if

---

[4] Annuity guarantees are based solely on the claims paying ability of the issuing company and compliance with product terms.

you're concerned the market is at such lofty peaks and wondering when the other shoe will drop, it makes sense to speak with an expert. You're thinking about it – it's time to act.

But you're probably too busy, right? I get that, we're all busy. Some people think there's never a good time to talk retirement planning. I'm the opposite – I think it's always a good time to address your retirement. Most people spend more time planning a summer trip than their retirement. They're not too busy to plan a two-week vacation, but they are too busy to worry about planning 30 or more years of their lives.

Another reservation I see is people aren't sure they can do anything with their assets or they think they don't have enough. Well, without sitting down and talking, there's no way an expert will know either. In my experience, even smaller portfolios can benefit from working with a qualified financial professional.

People who are using their assets for retirement planning often already have "good" advisors and brokers they swear by. If that's true, people like me will be the first to tell them that. It becomes pretty clear in our financial review when there is a good fit because your plan meets your goals.

If you think your advisor is great, then it's a perfect time to seek a second opinion. You'll either receive validation that your plan is sound and on-track, or, news that it isn't. If you hear the latter, it could be down to the expert(s) you're working with.

I see more than 800 people every year. I can count on one hand the number of people who have all their i's dotted, all their t's crossed, and are in really good shape. If you are one of those folks, I'll say that you're solid and you shouldn't change anything. You would leave with that much more confidence in your advisor. If your plan isn't in great shape, you'll have options in front of you to get it there.

Many times, the problems I see in people's plans come down to misalignment, like we talked about in Chapter Three. While people don't usually come out and say it, it's clear by their behavior that they don't want to align their assets.

I've had the good fortune and blessing of being interviewed by media outlets during my career. One I remember was for a feature on Fox Business News – the interview lasted four hours. During it, they asked me to identify the single biggest mistake retirement savers make. I said it was that people are out of alignment.

The reporter asked what that meant. I said people come into my office all the time saying their top priority is they want their money protected. When we review their statements, the bulk of the money is in the stock market. So they're telling me one thing, but their account reflects the exact opposite. And they wonder why every eight years or so they lose half their money. It's because they're out of alignment. And my job is to get people in alignment for good.

Fox liked that answer so much, it was featured in a nationwide clip.

Another reservation people have is the fear of being burned again because someone they trusted did them wrong in the past. I certainly understand that; it's happened to me too.

Couldn't we all say that about some walk of life? I can't be the only one who's had a bad experience with an auto mechanic. When it happened to me, it was really bad because the mechanic was also my brother.

The truth is there are bad people in every industry, mine included. I'm sure you've heard the horror stories. But I have a news flash – we're not all bad. In fact, some of us actually help people. Vet a potential financial professional with tough questions. Before you commit, make sure you know who you're working with.

All the reservations I've mentioned lead to one thing – inaction. And as I discussed last chapter, there is a hefty opportunity cost to be paid for inaction.

I hold seminars regularly in various parts of Pennsylvania, Delaware, and Maryland. In any given year, I'll do 45 or more seminars that attract up to 60 people each. I don't say this to impress you, but rather to illustrate how, every week, people sit in the audience and still don't act. Someone sat there in 2008 and said they were too busy, that they'd have to think about it. And you, the reader of this book, may react in the same way.

Like those people back in 2008, it could cost your portfolio quite a bit to sit back and do nothing. This is especially true if you're out of alignment. Some people lost 30-40% or more.

Now, many financial experts will give you a free consultative review – I certainly will. It won't cost you a dime. This is the first step to breaking the cycle of inaction. It will cost time, but that could be a down payment on a secure retirement.

Clearly, a safe retirement has a lot of moving parts, based on everything we've covered in this book. There is quite a lot people don't know about retirement that can hurt them. And, this book is only a slice of the whole pie.

There are several risks and lots of complexity involved with retirement planning, especially retirement income. Given this, wouldn't you say a free discussion about your situation with an expert is a sound investment?

Don't let procrastination, fear or a lack of knowledge stop you. All those hurdles can be overcome with the right expert guide. With quality professional help, you can avoid the many potential pitfalls in retirement and realize the life you want.

Chapter Eleven

The Secure Act Changes the American Retirement Game

The SECURE Act ushered in wholesale changes to American retirement, changing the game in the process. It was signed into law on December 20, 2019, as part of a $1.4 trillion spending bill to keep the government running (the SECURE Act was tucked inside this legislation). It's the most sweeping piece of retirement legislation since the Economic Recovery Tax Act of 1981.

The SECURE Act changed the game in several ways. For example, it eliminated the age limit for Traditional IRA and Roth IRA contributions. Under the old rules, if you were more than 70-and-a-half years old, you couldn't contribute. But now with the SECURE Act, if you are still working, you can contribute, regardless of your age.

But there's always a caveat.

In this case, it's that you must have earned income to contribute to a retirement account. That sounds easier than it really is because pension proceeds, Social Security, dividends, real estate sales, and more do not qualify as earned income.

We had a retired client who brought in his tax return, and I saw he had taken a $6,000 deduction on his return as a Traditional IRA contribution. I asked about it and he said after he did his taxes, he realized he owed the government some money. He then figured he'd throw $6,000 in an IRA to reduce his tax liability. In fact, after that, he was owed a bit of money from the government.

I congratulated him on his good planning and asked where he worked during the year. He said, "Work? I don't work. You know I'm retired."

I followed up, asking about part-time work, contracting, consulting, or something along those lines. His response was, "Dan, I have plenty of money and I don't need to work. I'm retired."

Unfortunately, I had to break some bad news to him. I told him if he was retired and didn't have any earned income, he couldn't contribute to a Traditional IRA account. I'll never forget his response. He said it should be fine because his tax software let him do it. So, I told him the software might be good with it, but the IRS won't be.

As you can imagine, he was a bit distraught and asked what he could do. I advised him to file an amended return, back out the IRA contribution, and pay what he owed. The government may not catch it this year or next year, but it would eventually. At that point, penalties and interest would make the amount owed a lot more than the original tax liability.

So, you can now contribute to an IRA beyond age 70-and-a-half, however, you must have earned income. Basically, you have to work. Whether it's a commission, a salary, or fees, somebody has to pay you to do something.

A second game changer in the SECURE Act is the minimum age to begin RMDs from retirement accounts is now 72, instead of 70-and-a-half. In a small way, I'm quite thankful for this because who can remember their 70th-and-a-half birthday? Nobody! That's surprising because it's only 11 years after your 59th-and-a-half birthday. Seriously, why not just 59 and 70? That's the government at work, I suppose.

Kidding aside, just like the previous rules, the beginning RMD date can be delayed until April 1 of the year following the year you reach age 72. However, we don't recommend that because then you have to take two RMDs that first year.

One positive effect of delaying the RMD age is a larger "sweet spot" for retirement planning. The "sweet spot" is that period of time when you can access your retirement money penalty-free after age 59-and-a-half and before you're required to take RMDs, now age 72.

You've got more flexibility now between those years to decide what tax bracket you're going to be in, potentially do Roth IRA conversions, and more. In other words, the SECURE Act provides a bigger opportunity to take advantage of historically low tax rates. Done right, this sort of tax and income planning can make a really big difference in retirement.

For IRA owners and beneficiaries who are charitably inclined, the SECURE Act didn't change much – call it a game-maintainer. But that's noteworthy in and of itself because of the other changes the law did make.

Qualified charitable distributions from retirement accounts are popular for people looking to use the standard tax deduction and still get a break for a charitable contribution. These kinds of distributions are still available at age 70-and-a-half (not age 72). This is important to keep in mind for retirement planning – you must know the rules and when they apply.

There is one last item to note on the charity front. If you're thinking about making deductible contributions to a Traditional IRA at age 70-and-a-half or older *and* considering a qualified charitable distribution, proceed with caution. Congress has a complicated formula that can limit the tax break available with a charitable deduction. To simplify this scenario, consider making a Roth IRA contribution instead, bypassing taxes altogether.

Another item in the SECURE Act that may not generate many headlines, though it's a potentially big change, is annuities may become more widely available in qualified workplace retirement plans. That means

401(k) plans and the like can offer annuities alongside other investment options. This is great news for people seeking guaranteed income. Still, annuities can be complex, so getting professional help makes a lot of sense, even if it's within your employer retirement plan.

Another, perhaps unexpected, set of winners under the SECURE Act are families (or those looking to start them). The law allows penalty-free distributions from retirement accounts for births or adoptions.

Normally, if you're under age 59-and-a-half and take a distribution from a retirement account, you're subject to a 10% penalty and income taxes. The SECURE Act allows a $5,000 distribution for birth or adoption without a penalty. However, taxes would still be owed.

This provision applies to both IRAs and employer plans but is limited to $5,000 for each birth or adoption. To qualify, the distribution has to be taken within one year from the date of birth or date when the adoption was finalized.

So, a married couple could each take a $5,000 distribution ($10,000 total) without penalty from their retirement plans following the birth or adoption of a child. There's no requirement to use the money for birth or adoption expenses. Also, the distribution amount could be recontributed back to the account(s) at any future time.

It's a nice benefit, don't get me wrong. However, I would advise most folks that retirement accounts are for retirement. Still, circumstances may deem a retirement account be used for something else as a last resort. Just understand there are long-term costs associated with early withdrawals.

The SECURE Act gamechangers mentioned so far will undoubtedly impact American retirement. But the law's biggest impact will surely be the elimination of the "stretch" IRA. That was a retirement strategy that enabled "stretching" a retirement account over multiple lifetimes.

Well, goodbye "stretch" IRA and hello 10-year liquidation period. Before I explain all that, I'd like to quickly illustrate the power of a "stretch" IRA.

Say a grandparent named their only grandchild as the sole beneficiary on a $100,000 IRA. Let's assume the grandchild was a year old and was fortunate enough to earn an 8% annual return on the account.

Why the grandchild? Let's be honest, if the grandparent was like most of us, they probably like their grandchild better than their own kid!

Under the old law, when do you think that grandchild would have to start taking RMDs? Most people say 72, but that's incorrect. The grandchild must take RMDs beginning at age 2 (a year after the account was inherited).

Keep in mind, the RMDs would be small. That's because the old law allowed for RMDs to be taken over the lifespan of the inherited account owner. As you can imagine, in actuarial terms the average lifespan of a 1-year-old is quite long. So out of the $100,000 balance, the RMD would be slightly more than $1,200.

The 8% annual gain would cover that easily, meaning the overall account balance would grow.

If that scenario played out over the average lifespan of a human (roughly 83 years), the initial $100,000 IRA would turn out to be worth more than $8 million! If it occurred within a Roth IRA, the entire account value would be tax-free.

Year	Age	IRA Value	RMD	RMD total
2004	1	$100,000	$1,225	$1,225
2013	10	$177,852	$2,450	$17,753
2023	20	$331,083	$5,289	$56,079
2033	30	$600,605	$11,418	$138,825
2043	40	$1,050,147	$24,651	$317,470
2053	50	$1,734,988	$53,220	$703,152
2063	60	$2,596,717	$114,899	$1,535,812
2073	70	$3,125,533	$248,058	$3,333,463
2083	80	$1,392,402	$535,539	$7,214,455
2084	81	$925,412	$578,383	$7,792,838
2085	82	$374,791	$374,791	$8,167,629
2086	83	$0	$0	$8,167,629
Courtesy of Ed Slott, CPA, © 2006, used with permission				

Isn't that amazing?

Yes, it *was*.

The "stretch" IRA was so amazing, the government got rid of it! It's probably a bit clearer now why the law changed – Uncle Sam wants his cut in exchange for the many years of tax breaks.

Beginning for deaths after Dec. 31, 2019, the "stretch" IRA was replaced with a 10-year liquidation rule for the vast majority of beneficiaries. This new rule requires inherited accounts to be emptied by the end of the tenth year following the year of death.

There are no annual RMDs. Instead, the only real RMD on an inherited IRA is the balance must be $0 at the end of 10 years after death. This rule applies to beneficiaries of both Traditional and Roth IRAs.

What if you inherited an IRA before 2020? The old rules remain in place. That means you can continue to "stretch" if you are the beneficiary of such an account.

However, if that account is passed on again, the "stretch" ends. In such a case, any successor beneficiary on an inherited account is subject to the 10-year rule under the SECURE Act.

For example, say I inherited an IRA from my father in 2019. I have the lifetime benefit of the "stretch" IRA. However, if I die with money left in the account and it goes to my kids, they'll be subject to the 10-year rule.

So, does the 10-year rule apply to all beneficiaries? No. There are five classes of eligible designated beneficiaries who are exempt from the 10-year post-death payout rule. These people can still stretch RMDs over their respective life expectancies. They include:

1. Surviving spouses
2. Minor children (not grandchildren)
3. Disabled people
4. Chronically ill people
5. Beneficiaries not more than 10 years younger than the owner

If you're an eligible designated beneficiary, you can still stretch the inherited IRA over your life expectancy. But keep in mind that once you no longer qualify, the 10-year rule applies.

Consider the case of minor children (not grandchildren) who qualify as eligible designated beneficiaries under the SECURE Act. They can "stretch" the RMDs until they no longer qualify, which would be when they're no longer a minor (in most states, age 18), or if they're in school, up until age 26. After that, the 10-year liquidation rule applies.

Say a parent died and left an IRA to their first grader. The child can stretch the RMDs until age 18 (or 26 if in school). But after that, the 10-year rule applies.

Unfortunately, these rules also apply to Roth IRAs – as if people need more reasons to be upset with the government. So even inherited Roth IRAs must be emptied within 10 years, per the SECURE Act.

I've had clients over the years, before the SECURE Act, who did fairly large Roth conversions with the idea that they'd never need the money. They planned to pass it on to their kids, who could then enjoy a tax-free income stream over the rest of their lives. Sadly, these folks had the rug pulled out from underneath them by Uncle Sam.

The "stretch" IRA *was* one of the best wealth transfer tools out there, whether Traditional or Roth IRA. If someone left a $1 million IRA, their kids could have an income the rest of their lives.

Not anymore.

My clients who paid the tax up front when doing Roth conversions figured the money could last their kids' entire lives. But now, the accounts must be emptied in a decade.

Of course, my clients were livid. They questioned why the government cared since the affected accounts were tax-free Roth IRAs. Why did it matter when the money came out?

I definitely saw their point of view. If I were in their situation, I would be upset too. But I also understand where the government is coming from, even if I disagree with its position. Essentially, the government wants to cut the heads off the geese laying the tax-free eggs. As a result, the possibility of tax-free gains for decades is going away.

Of course, this will create problems.

Consider this situation – a single parent died in 2020 and left an $800,000 IRA to their 30-year-old daughter. The SECURE Act's 10-year rule applies, so what's the strategy for the daughter?

Well, if it's a Traditional IRA, the strategy ought to be to withdraw 10% per year over a decade. Keep in mind, she doesn't have to take anything out. But at the end of a decade, say the IRA is worth $1.2 million. She would then have to take all that out in one year, getting slaughtered on the taxes.

So, the strategy with a Traditional IRA would be to take out 10% per year. This would get the account shut down in 10 years paying the least amount of taxes.

If someone inherits a Traditional IRA and doesn't understand that basic concept, they're probably in trouble. These folks could very well end up needlessly paying income taxes on millions of dollars. I consider that a problem and I bet anyone who must pay those tax bills will too.

Now, the strategy with an inherited Roth IRA is the opposite. There is no tax bill at the end of the liquidation period. So, let it grow as much as possible. In the same $800,000 IRA scenario, let it grow to $1.2 million because it will all come out tax-free.

But here's where the problem lies. I'll use myself as an example. Say I had $1 million in an IRA and left it all to my four children since, in this example, my wife predeceased me. Now let's say I live for a while longer, making it to about 80 years old, before each of my kids gets $250,000.

At that point, my kids would range in age from 50-55. These are often the peak earning years for an adult, so they'll probably be earning some of the highest wages they'll ever earn. While the $250,000 from my IRA is nice, do they want to add that on top of their peak earnings and push their income tax liabilities through the roof? They would lose a lot of that money to taxes.

But there's good news. Under the SECURE Act, they have 10 years to withdraw the money. And there are no RMDs. So, my kids might figure they'll go another 10 years, retire, and be in a lower tax bracket.

But plans don't always work as intended. Fast forward 10 years, and guess what? Life got in the way.

While life was happening – vacations, weddings, work, this, that, and the other thing – that 10-year deadline passed, and time marched on. Meanwhile, the $250,000 grew to $500,000.

So, they've missed the liquidation deadline under the SECURE Act, which is the only true RMD, and the accounts have doubled to $500,000. Do you remember the penalty on a missed RMD? It's 50%!

In such a case, my kids would then have to liquidate the accounts ($500,000 each) and pay a 50% penalty ($250,000 each) for missing the RMDs. They'd also be liable for income taxes, which would probably be somewhere around a 40% levy ($200,000 each).

Where's does that leave them?

After more than a decade, they lost 90% of the value of the IRA to penalties and taxes. In other words, they turned $500,000 into $50,000 and didn't even have to step into a casino to do it.

Could you see that becoming commonplace across America? I could. People will forget about the rules, and this situation will play out time after time, creating big problems down the road.

And those who think having a trust as a Traditional IRA beneficiary will save them from the SECURE Act are incorrect. The law applies to most trusts as well, so many trusts will no longer work as planned. If money is paid out of the trust, it could result in large, taxable distributions. Conversely, if money is kept in the trust, it could produce high trust tax rates.

As a result, the SECURE Act makes leaving a Roth IRA to a trust more beneficial than leaving a Traditional IRA. But achieving that can take some work if you already have a plan in place. If you're in this type of situation, your plan needs an immediate review and likely overhaul.

Such is the ripple effect of the SECURE Act. With the elimination of the "stretch" IRA, estate planning has been greatly affected. What was for many years a stellar wealth transfer tool has weakened.

But a new go-to way to transfer wealth has emerged – life insurance. Since the payouts are tax-free, life insurance is as efficient as it gets.

Let's say you set up a $250,000 life insurance policy for your kids. That gives you a clean conscience to spend every last dollar you have. Because in the end, the kids are going to get $250,000 to split tax-free from a life insurance policy.

All right, we've covered a lot.

Let's take a breath and wrap it all up.

Before the SECURE Act, Americans had proven retirement and estate planning strategies to rely on. But the new law has changed the game in so many ways (we've covered some in this chapter), that new strategies are required.

Still, the key question remains the same – how will it affect you?

Well, there may be new opportunities to make IRA contributions. You may be able to access retirement funds without penalty. Delaying RMDs a bit longer is possible and may make sense.

And that's just a small bit of the pie.

You'll certainly need to give serious consideration to how the elimination of the "stretch" IRA will impact you and your beneficiaries. Speaking of IRA beneficiaries, it's a good idea to review those in case you need to make updates.

The SECURE Act might mean converting Traditional IRA assets to a Roth IRA is part of the plan now. In the context of estate planning, we've already seen how the type of IRA account matters for beneficiaries.

Another estate planning move could be to increase the use of life insurance. The tax-free payouts are attractive and can deliver peace of mind, which always helps.

All these strategies are worth evaluating in the wake of the SECURE Act. But as you've probably realized – it can be quite complex. So now more than ever, good guidance is essential. A qualified advisor can guide you through all the new rules, helping ensure you're in the best position to take advantage of the breaks while avoiding the dangers.

In this new retirement frontier, many strategies and plans changed because the rules changed. The thing is, one of the biggest problems is some advisors don't know the rules. It can't be said enough – getting quality help is essential.

The following story occurred before the SECURE Act, when "stretch" IRAs were still possible. But the principle remains as true as ever – you must know the rules.

We had a client, a woman who was about 80 years old, who died and left an IRA worth about $400,000 to her sister. Our client wasn't married and didn't have any children, so she left the account to her sister.

My team set up an inherited IRA that the sister could "stretch" over her life expectancy. Well, six months later, I get a statement saying the sister's account is empty. So, I called her and asked what happened.

She said she met another advisor who told her she could do better with them and decided to move the account. I told her that was not a problem and asked if the account was transferred directly or if she was sent a check. She said they sent a check. I then asked if she deposited it, which she did – the day before.

Uh oh.

I hated to tell her, but I had to level with her – depositing that $400,000 check was a taxable action. In other words, she was on the hook for income taxes because she just "made" $400,000 of income.

She said her advisor told her she had 60 days to roll the money into another IRA account. Again, I had to correct her (and her mistaken advisor). If that were her IRA originally, she would be correct. But it was her sister's IRA, not hers. When transferring an inherited IRA, it must go from custodian to custodian. If it touches your hands, it becomes taxable.

After relaying all this, I thought she was going to cry. It's not easy finding out your nest egg shrunk by 40% and you suddenly owe $160,000 to Uncle Sam.

The sad part is, advisors don't always know the rules, but everyday people are the ones who end up suffering. What makes the problem worse is the rules are always changing.

The SECURE Act is a perfect example. So many game changers! And yet, one constant remains – you must know the rules to take advantage of the breaks while avoiding the dangers.